Rhodesian Legacy

Rhodesian Legacy

Photographs
IAN MURPHY

Text
ALF WANNENBURGH

GALAXIE PRESS (PVT) LTD
SALISBURY ZIMBABWE RHODESIA 1979

This edition published by Galaxie Press 1979.

First published in 1978
by C. Struik Publishers, 56 Wale Street, Cape Town.

Copyright © Text and captions: C. Struik Publishers.
Copyright © Photographs: Ian Murphy.

ISBN 0 86925 097 3

Shona proverbs appear by courtesy of Mambo Press,
Gwelo, Zimbabwe Rhodesia.

Designed by Walther Votteler, Cape Town.
Typography by Wim Reinders, Cape Town.
Photoset by McManus Bros. (Pty) Limited, Cape Town.
Lithographic reproduction by Unifoto (Pty) Limited,
Cape Town.
Printed and bound by Printopac, a Division of
Rhodesia Packing (Pvt.) Ltd.,
Salisbury, Zimbabwe Rhodesia.

Acknowledgements

As a photographer out in the field, one is indebted to many people for their kindness and assistance. I would like to thank all those who have helped, specifically my parents whose sense of adventure inspired this project; the Shaws of Penhalonga; Jeff Stutchbury of Bumi Hills Safari Lodge, whose help and understanding made the Kariba section possible; and Allan Elliot of Wankie Safari Lodge whose intoxicating enthusiasm and knowledge of his environment has, I hope, come through in the Wankie section. Finally I would like to thank Tom Bloomfield, Peter Forrest-Smith and Mike Gardner in Salisbury and Walter and Sue Ferrier in Cape Town.

Contents

ZAMBIA

MAP OF RHODESIA

MOÇAMBIQUE

Zambezi

Chirundu

Kariba

Karoi

Over 1 000 metres

Over 1 300 metres

MATUSADONA
NATIONAL PARK

Lake Kariba

0   50   100

Kilometres

Sinoia

SALISBURY

CHIZARIRA
NATIONAL PARK

Marandellas

Victoria Falls

Zambezi

Gatooma

Rusape

INYANGA

Penhalonga

Wankie

Sabi

Que Que

Enkeldoorn

UMTALI

WANKIE NATIONAL PARK

VUMBA

GWELO

Cashel

Selukwe

Melsetter

Birchenough Bridge

Fort Victoria

BULAWAYO

Lake Kyle

Chipinga

CHIMANIMANI

Plumtree

Shabani

Zimbabwe Ruins

Cecil Rhodes Grave

RHODES MATOPOS
NATIONAL PARK

Gwanda

Sabi

Chiredzi

GONA-RE-ZHOU
NATIONAL PARK

BOTSWANA

Shashi

Beitbridge

Limpopo

Limpopo

MOÇAMBIQUE

REPUBLIC OF SOUTH AFRICA

Time Perspective

Nhasi haasiri mangwana
Today is not tomorrow *Shona proverb*

Of some seven million people who live today in the land which lies between the Limpopo and Zambezi rivers, the Kalahari Desert and the lowveld of Moçambique, no more than a handful of nomadic hunter-gatherers living on the edge of the desert can claim genetic and cultural descent from its earliest *Homo sapiens* inhabitants. All the rest of the people living in what is now Rhodesia are heirs to pioneers and conquerors, colonisers and immigrants – black and white. While ancestral kin of most of them were already in this land in the first millennium A.D., the roots of some have scarcely pierced the topsoil of the present century. But, once penetrated, this land takes hold of root and soul in a grip as firm at surface as at bedrock.

Successive conquerors and assimilators have become in turn conquered and assimilated. Rhodesia is a land peopled by the residues of vanished empires. The past periods of their ascendency are measured in centuries and less. Beside them, the land itself, its changes spanning hundreds of millions of years, seems eternal.

Only 90-odd years have passed since Cecil John Rhodes gazed northwards from the Cape of Good Hope and roused young men to seek their fortunes, and his, in the land which later would be named after him. And already the heirs of these same young men, who founded Rhodesia for 'justice, freedom and commerce' under the British South Africa Company, are facing a future quite unlike the one they thought they were building for themselves in this same land.

Half a century before Rhodes's young men arrived, the Ndebele under Mzilikazi, moving west like a shock wave from the eruption of the Zulu Kingdom in what is today South Africa, were deflected northward across the Limpopo by the Boers. In the land that was to become Rhodesia they imposed their dominion over the Shona, heirs to dynasties that had ruled over varying portions of the territory for 1 500 years.

Still earlier, the forefathers of the Cape Hottentots had also passed this way on their long migration from the north-east. And the Bushmen, who had occupied the land alone with the animals for several thousand years, recorded these events in paint on the granite walls of their caves and rock shelters.

For upward of 50 000 years, men had been chipping away at stones, fashioning implements among the hills and in the valleys of the land which Rhodes would some day claim for Queen Victoria. Their techniques developed, the size and pattern of their artefacts changed, and it is according to these changes in their material culture that they are classified today. Their skeletal remains have not been uncovered to reveal what sort of men they were. A single skull unearthed north of the Zambezi suggests that 35 000 years ago 'Rhodesian Man' was a humanoid closer to modern man than was his European Neanderthal contemporary. But only the worked stone fragments left behind bear witness to man's evolution here; the land has not disclosed its secrets.

Like totems and national flags, the name given by a people to their territory is treated with reverence and often defended with their blood. The name symbolises for them a perpetual present, a way of life they assume will last forever – which it never does.

In the perspective of earth-time, names like Zimbabwe, Rhodesia, Matabeleland, Mashonaland, Manyika, Changamire and Monomatapa are more like sub-titles for short sequences, perhaps only a few frames, in a documentary movie without visible beginning or end, winding out of the conjectured past into the inscrutable future. From time to time, new human figures appear briefly on the flickering screen, to live and love, wage war and multiply. Then the images pale, figures in bolder colours are superimposed, and another 'perpetual present' vanishes beyond memory under ever more layers of film on the take-up reel.

Names change, statues are pulled down, but the land, its people and their positive works live on under a new identity. They are the legacy of the imperfectly understood past to the barely conceived future. The past, the Shona say, does not remain the past – '*Kare haagari ari kare*'.

7

Legacy of the Granite Hills

The peacefulness of it all; the chaotic grandeur. It creates a feeling of awe and brings home to us how very small we are. Cecil John Rhodes

'Long, long ago, when the stones were still soft . . .', the Ndebele say when they speak of the age of myth and fable, when Somandhla, also called Nkulunkulu, the Great Great One, moulded the laws of nature and of man.

Long, long ago, when the stones were still soft, the first men sent Nwabu, the chameleon, and Ntuli, the lizard, as messengers to Somandhla: the chameleon to ask that man be given eternal life; the lizard to request his mortality. The chameleon lingered on the way and the lizard reached the Great Great One first. And so today, Ndebele children still take their revenge on the lizard because he was too quick, and the chameleon for being too slow. But they cannot alter the fact of their mortality, because it was written into the laws of nature before the rocks were hard.

Rocks crumble and become the soil which, together with climate, lays down which plants may grow, which animals may feed and flourish, what kind of life is possible for man.

Much of the human story over the last 2 000 years in this land between the Zambezi and the Limpopo has been associated with some of the oldest rock formations on earth. These ancient schists yielded the gold which the first black immigrants from the north traded with the Middle and Far East as early as the second century A.D. It was gold that built the stone walls of Great Zimbabwe and laid the foundations of the later Monomatapa and Changamire dynasties. Gold drew the Portuguese up the Zambezi Valley and through the Eastern Highlands from the coast. Its lustre also caught the eye of Cecil John Rhodes and brought the British. But gold, although still an important mineral, is no longer such a vital factor in the country's economy. Rhodesia's vast reserves of strategic metals are what interest the super powers of today.

Gold and strategic metals meant nothing, however, to the Late Stone Age Bushmen, who were in the country all those thousands of years before the black men and white men came. They chose to live chiefly in areas where weathering, over more than 3 000 million years, had exposed portions of the granite shield which had crystallised beneath the surface of the whole country.

The largest area of exposed granite is the Matopo Hills, in the south-west. Here the alternating heat of day and chill of night fractured and broke up the surface of the shield. Where natural lines of weakness in the rock were close together, temperature fluctuation left the towering stacks of balancing rounded granite cubes of every size that today are called 'castle kopjes'. Where the weaknesses were further apart, it flenched the massive 'whaleback' dwalas, stripping off even layers of rock, leaving here and there a sentinel group of giant boulders on a summit. A similar process hollowed out the domed caves which would become lairs for leopards, retreats for baboons and shelters for early men.

The mountain acacia, lucky bean tree and Cape chestnut, the tree fern and candelabra tree took root in the residual granite soil in the valleys, and brilliant orange and pale green lichens spread their lacework over rockfaces. The leguan, the python and the black mamba appeared. So too did ostrich, rhino, giraffe, buffalo, zebra, wildebeest, kudu, eland and sable antelope. Rock rabbits scuttled in the crevices and black eagles nested high on jointed rock columns.

It was here that, perhaps 50 000 years ago, Middle Stone Age man left his small-flake tools. Here, some 30 000 years later, the Bushman lived in his 'golden age', remembered in his folklore as a time 'when men and animals spoke the same language'.

Tortoises were plentiful in the Matopos and the rock rabbits multiplied faster than he, the leopard and the black eagle together could eat them. After the rains, there was an abundance of roots and tubers, bulbs and berries. It was a natural paradise for the ecologically impeccable Bushman, who never gave a thought to conquering nature or taming the land, who put back what he took out at another point in the food chain. Bountiful nature afforded him time to contemplate, reflect and look again. And then he compounded the ochres of the veld with egg-white, fat, gum and urine, and on the walls of his caves he began painting what he saw.

Sympathetic magic, in which the imitation of natural objects is expected to have an effect on them, may have been one of the motives for his art, for he was careful to represent his own kind only in stylized form, so as not to harm them or have an influence on their lives. But empathetic magic, the enchantment he experienced in his unity with nature, must have inspired the naturalistic technique he refined to represent all else to perfection.

His first daubs were simple monochrome silhouettes of single animals that were static and lacked perspective. It took him a thousand years or more to discover all the secrets of representing movement, and a little more to mature his sense of line. Then he burst into a multi-coloured celebration of his world with paintings of everyday scenes: animals chiefly, vibrant and detailed, in sketched landscapes. He portrayed the transient ancestors of the Hottentots with the same attention to detail that he gave to all except his own people. Colour liberated great abstract compositions, and mythological beings began to take shape on his walls.

The Bushman seems to have lived in the state of mind aspired to by Eastern mystics, the 'eternal present', in which the past and the future exist only in the experience of the present moment. But the illusory 'perpetual present', in which the conditions of physical and cultural life appear to be permanent, was the same for the Bushman as for anyone else. And quite suddenly, it began to change. Strangers – black agriculturalists and cattle and sheep herders – entered the land and intruded upon his monistic cosmos. Their life-ways were incompatible, their world views clashed. Gradually, and then completely, the more powerful stranger either assimilated the Bushman or pushed him out into the wastelands. And, on the walls of caves he had vacated in his lost paradise, sheltering black herdboys now made crude copies in black and white of the paintings they called *madzimudzangara* – 'spirits of long ago'.

But the 'bald heads' of the Matopos, crowding some 3 000 square kilometres with natural domes and spires, retained their spiritual appeal. Five hundred years ago, a priest from Great Zimbabwe made a cave in the southern Matopos the centre of the Rozwi cult of the High God, Mwari – Lord of the Sky, the Great Pool, Creator of People, Provider of Good and Evil, Source of Thunder and Lightning, who existed from the very beginning. Here, at the start of the rainy season and after harvest, virgins danced, and cattle, grain and millet beer were offered in supplication and thanksgiving. Here, in adversity, the people came to consult the oracle, and the 'voice' answered them from the resonant darkness in an ancient dialect.

And when the battle-calloused Ndebele came up as conquerors from the south 140 years ago, they assimilated the Rozwi and Kalanga, adopted the Mwari cult

and treated the Matopos as sacred ground. Almost 60 years later, after they rebelled against the administration imposed on them by the British, these hills, in which their first king, Mzilikazi, had been buried, became their refuge. Without a king since Lobengula had died fleeing from the white men in the far north three years earlier, the Ndebele rallied around their oracle. When the Europeans discovered the holy rain cave, they moved the oracle to a succession of other caves, until eventually Rhodes persuaded them that the particular 'perpetual present' they had been living in could not resist the global process which he represented.

But even as dedicated an imperialist as Rhodes did not escape the enchantment of the Matopos. He felt the 'chaotic grandeur' of the hills humble him as he stood on the summit of one of the grandest of them; the one the Ndebele called Malindidzimu – Dwelling Place of the Spirits. It was here, among the guardian spirits of Mzilikazi, that he willed to be buried. But he renamed the hill, ensuring that, while in life he had been content to contemplate a continent, in death he would have a View of the World.

New spirits joined the Rhodesian pantheon on Malindidzimu. Leander Starr Jameson, the first administrator of Rhodesia, and Charles Patrick John Coghlan, its first prime minister, were buried here in crypts cut in the rock. The bones of Major Allan Wilson and his ill-fated Shangani Patrol, who fought to the last man when trapped by Lobengula's impis in a mopane forest north of the Shangani River, were brought from their earlier resting place at Great Zimbabwe and placed here in a bronze and granite monument inscribed 'To Brave Men'.

It is said that those of the patrol who were still alive just before the Ndebele's final assault removed their hats and sang *God Save the Queen*. There were no survivors.

More than 20 years ago Sir Robert Tredgold remarked in his book about these hills that an account of almost every incident of historical importance in the western part of the country seemed to lead back to the Matopos. Here the spiritual and heroic traditions of all the peoples of this land meet on common territory, for the hills are one of the ancient battlefields of Rhodesia, where the bones of fallen European, Ndebele and Shona warriors have mingled and become one with the earth. Here the spirits of Rhodesia's heroes live together with the tribal deities and departed spirits of the Ndebele, and the heirs of both of them to this day still honour the Shona spirits by sending tribute in times of crisis and thanksgiving to the sacred cave of the Mwari oracle.

9

In the lounge at the hotel, a party of art students from Salisbury talk about black eagles and a reunification of art and nature that will be grander than civilization.

At the reception desk, the manager slides a snub-nosed automatic pistol across the boards and says: 'You'd better take this with you if you're driving about in the hills on your own, but if you get revved by terrs, don't try to shoot it out with them. Put your foot down hard and return their fire through the window.'

He leaves by a different door each night when he closes up – avoiding fatal patterns.

'Early morning is the time to be at View of the World,' he says. 'You can watch the sun rise over the Shangani monument. Rhodes and Wilson mean a lot to us, especially now.'

Another Matopos twilight. Slanting sunlight dapples the long grass beside the road with shadows of possible menace. A mamba flows three metres long out of a thicket, forebody raised, scanning; incarnate Departed Spirit of the South, *Amadhlozi Ezansi*, protector of the nation.

From Rhodes's grave on Malindidzimu, National Parks scout Sidakwa Tomaisi has watched every sunrise and every sunset for 18 years. He has observed the changes of the hours, the seasons and the years. Eighteen times he has witnessed summer's greens, blues and magentas shade into winter's yellows, pinks, oranges and browns. His view of the world has dissolved all the illusory 'perpetual presents' into an 'eternal present'. He does not look for words to describe it.

Among the thousands of rainbow-coloured lizards that are his daily companions on top of Malindidzimu, he has outgrown his childhood dislike of Ntuli. They swarm about his feet when he calls them for the morsels of dry *sadza* porridge he brings them in his pockets. With his Shona colleagues he would say that no one thing is better than another – '*Hakuna chinonakira chimwe*'.

Lion Spirits of the High Plateau

Kugadzwa umambo / kugwadamira midzimu
To be made a chief is the reward for worshipping one's ancestor spirit *Shona proverb*

According to Shona fable, the Great God, Mwari, dispenser of nature's bounty to man, gave cattle and people to one man, while to another he gave only a handful of soil. But the man who received the soil became a great chief, while the other became a headman under him, for as owner of the soil he could claim all that grew in it and that was nurtured by it, crops, cattle and men. Thus sovereignty over the land is the source of chiefly authority. Once a man has been given the soil, no one else can be chief in his place for as long as he lives.

The high land lying between the Zambezi and the Limpopo is as good as any man could wish to have sovereignty over. The great earth-building forces which moulded the rocks also arched the foundations, creating over two-thirds of the country a high plateau with a climate uniquely congenial all year round.

Surrounded by regions which, at least at certain times of year, would be regarded by most people as uncomfortable, if not oppressive, the plateau stands out as a temperate island in South Central Africa, with altitudes rising from a little over 1 000 metres in the south-west to above 2 500 metres in the north-east. On either side of this main watershed the land falls away gently towards the two great rivers. Elevation limits maximum temperatures on the plateau to between 20° and 30° Celsius throughout the year, and the thunderstorms that march over the land on summer afternoons provide from 600 to 1 000 millimetres of rain annually. And after the rains have fallen, the msasa trees put out their new red leaves and the grass stands green and shoulder high

It was perfect country for the black stockmen and agriculturalists who were moving southward in search of new territory, but a broad band of hot, dry lowveld barred their way. Here, in the shadows of the dense bush, swarmed the tsetse fly, carrier of trypano-somiasis, the dreaded sleeping sickness that was fatal to cattle and debilitating to man. And what good was the tall grass to a cattleman who had lost all his stock in trying to reach it? How could the fertile soil profit a man who no longer had the strength to till it?

And so, for many centuries, the tsetse fly was the Rhodesian Bushman's last bastion against strangers encroaching on his paradise.

Once a Shona chief has accepted his handful of soil from Mwari, he cannot relinquish his responsibility for the land it symbolises and all that is nurtured by it, even after death.

The land belongs to the living and the dead, but more so to the dead than to the living. All men join their ancestors when they die, and their respon-sibilities in the spirit world are an extension of their earthly ones. In the spirit world a dead chief becomes a *mhondoro*, a lion spirit, guardian of the land and those who live on it. When the living need his assistance, he appears among them at a séance, taking possession of the man who is his recognised spirit medium, speaking to them with the medium's tongue, but not in his voice.

When the lion spirits roar, the earth trembles. Nobody today knows what the first immigrants from the north who found fly-free corridors through the lowveld called themselves. From such traces of their material culture as have been found, it is known what parts of the plateau they inhabited and it is possible to form some idea of what sort of men they were. But the names they are known by today are the names of the sites where their cultural remains were first exten-sively excavated by archaeologists: Gokomere, north-west of Fort Victoria; and Ziwa, in the Inyanga district of the Eastern Highlands.

Cultural similarities suggest that they were related peoples who built houses for themselves of poles and anthill clay, planted sorghum and millet, kept many sheep and few cattle, fired clay pots and shallow bowls with decorated rims and shoulders, and hunted the elephant for its tusks.

The Gokomere people arrived on the plateau in the first century. By the middle of the second century they had established sporadic trade with the East Coast, exchanging ivory, copper and gold for sea shells, chi-na, cloth and glass beads with Asian merchants. Main-stay of this early commerce was the Indian demand for African ivory, which did not crack or splinter when carved. It was only some centuries later, when the Swahili intermediaries with the Arab world established themselves on the coast, that gold from the interior became the major article of trade, but by then the Gokomere people had faded from the scene.

They were the first Iron Age people to occupy briefly the hill at Great Zimbabwe, hundreds of years before the first stone walls were built there. In time, they spread westward into present-day Matabeleland and probed north-west into parts of Botswana and south across the Limpopo into the Transvaal. But by the ninth century, those of them who remained on the plateau had been absorbed by later black immigrants from the north.

And the Ziwa people, whose earliest traces date from the fourth century, fanned out over the territory from Inyanga across Mashonaland to beyond the site of the modern city of Salisbury. They cultivated small secluded valleys among granite hills and fashioned a distinctively patterned pottery that was still being made in this area in the eleventh century.

When a Shona community moves from its ancestral soil to a new territory, its tribal lion spirits do not move with it. They remain in the land which Mwari origi-nally placed under their guardianship. After a time, people settling in a new place develop spirit lineages of their own, but even then the lingering 'stranger' spirits of former inhabitants, who have been there longer, continue to have a powerful influence on events. The new people come to terms with them by giving them prominent places in the new ancestral pantheon, because they know that often the most potent spirits are 'strangers' from dynasties so old that even their names have been forgotten.

This is why, when things go wrong for people who are not attuned to the peculiarities of a new place, they say: 'We do not know the spirits of the land.'

Houses of Stone

Maunga marema / kudya muti waagere
Hairy caterpillars are stupid, they eat the trees
they live on *Shona proverb*

The easterly winds that prevail over the plateau originate far out in the Indian Ocean, but they carry little moisture to the interior. Most of it is shed in the coastal lowlands of Moçambique and against the uppermost windward slopes of Manicaland, on the eastern border. The wind drawn up through the Sabi River Valley spurns the south-eastern lowveld it passes over and favours with light showers and drizzle the places where the rise from the lowveld to the plateau is abrupt, as it is at Great Zimbabwe.

It is not difficult to imagine why the granite hills south of present-day Fort Victoria were so attractive 1 000 years ago to the succession of black migrants whose culture culminated eventually in the creation of the stone city of Great Zimbabwe. Not only was rainfall plentiful, but grazing was good, and the light granite soils in the valleys were easy to cultivate. The lower slopes of the hills were thickly covered with timber for building and burning, and the countryside around abounded in wild fruit and small game.

This was also the most suitable place for a great commercial centre to develop after the gold trade between the plateau peoples and the Swahili states on the coast burgeoned in the tenth century. Between the gold mining regions and the Sabi River Valley, which provided the least difficult and most direct route from the plateau to the coast, Zimbabwe was the furthest east that permanent human settlement was possible at that time. Beyond Great Zimbabwe the ground falls away sharply into the hot, dry lowveld, where the tsetse fly then ruled.

The centre of the Great Zimbabwe valley is dominated by a massive granite hill, with a sheer 30-metre cliff face along its crest and colossal boulders stacked on its eastern shoulder. Towards the west, the boulders are linked by stone walls which create enclosed spaces that are connected by open passages and, finally, a narrow covered stairway, to a larger area. This Western Enclosure, as it is called, is surrounded by a stone wall, seven metres thick at its base, tapering to four on top, and built on one side at the very edge of the cliff.

From the valley below and from the steep Ancient Ascent in the shadow of the wall, a Western eye sees superficial similarities to a medieval castle. And the expectation of a feudal estate seems to be fulfilled by the view from the parapet of the lush parkland in the valley, where the tall grass is threaded with the crumbling walls of lesser ruins and dotted with clumps of soft-leaved combretum, cabbage tree, lucky bean tree, common red milkwood and Cape fig – mumpembera, mufenje, mutiti, muchechete and mukuyu.

A cloud darkens the valley, and half a kilometre away, in a raised level clearing, the ten-metre high stone wall of the great Elliptical Enclosure shimmers white, pink and pale green, spotlit by a shaft of sunlight, like some mythical walled city. *Aloes excelsa* lurk giant-like among the lesser ruins, and the grass has the scent of freshly cut hay.

The Zimbabwe Ruins inspired their first nineteenth century European visitors to embark on even greater flights of fancy. This was the ruined Kingdom of Ophir, which had supplied King Solomon with 'gold and silver, ivory, and apes and peacocks'. The ruin on the hill was 'a copy of Solomon's Temple on Mount Moriah, and the building on the plain is a copy of the palace where the Queen of Sheba lived during her visit to Solomon' enthused the German geologist, Carl Mauch, who wrote the first eye-witness account of the ruins, but was deterred by an overgrowth of nettles from examining them closely. Cecil John Rhodes who, to stimulate interest in his projects north of the Limpopo, kept one of the eight stylised soapstone birds pilfered from the ruins, proclaimed them the ruins of 'an old Phoenician residence'. He suggested that the Bible be amended to read 'green parrots' for 'peacocks'. 'To think that the place . . . was once the abode of thousands of white men!' exclaimed D. C. de Waal, a member of the Cape Parliament who visited the Ruins with Rhodes. And Sir Rider Haggard wove the legend of King Solomon's Mines.

Victorian romantics named the ruin on the hill and the elliptical building in the valley The Acropolis and The Temple. Between 1896 and 1902, prospectors of Rhodesian Ancient Ruins Limited, who were licensed to ransack these sites for gold, regarded the stratified layers of soil containing the record of African occupation as the litter of later squatters, and the first curator

12

of the Ruins cast this irretrievable record aside as 'kaffir filth and decadence' in his quest for exotica.

There are almost 200 stone ruin sites on the central plateau, many of which the Shona today speak of as stone houses, *dzimba dzemabwe*, or venerated houses, *dzimba woye*. The first of them was built many centuries after the last Phoenician voyages of trade and discovery, and all belong to a progressive indigenous building tradition which began before the Arabs became prominent on the coast and ended at Great Zimbabwe before the Portuguese appeared in the Indian Ocean. Few of these sites are large and none can compare with the 12 separate clusters of buildings spread over 40 hectares at Great Zimbabwe.

Guidebooks keep alive the Victorian 'mystery' by favouring the vague 'final theory' that the Ruins are 'relatively late Southern African aspects of megalithic building, terraced cultivation and ancient mining traceable to original sources in the Near East'. But modern archaeologists and prehistorians, using scientific methods, have pieced together a far more engaging story.

According to recent findings, the site of Great Zimbabwe had no permanent inhabitants for some 500 years after the Gokomere people ended their short stay there in the fourth century. Then an oracle established a shrine in a cave at the eastern end of the hill, where words spoken in a normal voice could be heard clearly in the valley below.

In the ninth or tenth century another wave of black immigrants from the north settled in the south and south-west of the plateau, where they planted cereal crops, herded their cattle and mined iron, copper and gold. They were ancestral to the Kalanga who live in the south-west and north-west of the country, just as the people who built their huts of poles and anthill clay on the hill at Great Zimbabwe at about the same time, were ancestral to the Karanga in that region.

The new occupants of the hill were not the people who first built there in stone, however. Towards the end of the eleventh century yet another culturally related but better organised group, believed to have been the Rozwi, gained ascendency on the hill. They built sturdier homes for themselves which had thick clay walls with smooth surfaces. And then they began breaking up the evenly exfoliated granite shells they found in the vicinity into brick-sized blocks and started building walls with them.

The new rulers of Zimbabwe used the mystical sanctions of the oracle on their hill as an instrument of social control for organising the labour of the local people, so that they could derive maximum advantage from being situated where they could control the coastal trade route. The profits went into enhancing the status of their homes with walled enclosures.

By the end of the thirteenth century, extension of building into the valley was a sign that a growing number of men could afford this luxury. Trade stimulated local crafts based on raw materials from distant places. Gold was moulded into beads and beaten into leaf, cotton was spun and woven, soapstone was transformed into carvings, and iron was fashioned into hoes, axes and chisels for export. Beads, cowrie shells, brass rods and glazed Chinese, Persian and Near Eastern ceramics were imported from the coast in return.

Great Zimbabwe had grown to become the capital of an extensive trading empire, drawing tribute from distant communities, which were locally administered by the king's relatives, who lived in small stone-walled enclosures scattered about the central plateau. Archaeologists have identified some 60 of these as belonging to the style and period.

At the capital the skill of the builders was refined in the construction of the outer wall of the Elliptical Enclosure and climaxed in the chevron pattern built into the upper courses of its south-east-facing exterior. Their ultimate creation, a stone 'tower' in the shape of a traditional Shona grain bin, probably symbolised the king's status as owner of all the land and rightful recipient of tribute from its produce.

On the face of it, the people of Zimbabwe had every reason for supposing that the process of growth and enrichment would go on indefinitely, but there came a time in the fifteenth century when they felt suddenly that they no longer knew the spirits of the land. Their subsistence cultivation was unable to support so many people who were not engaged in food production. The soil became impoverished, their sources of salt were exhausted, the grazing became inadequate for their herds, the nearest timber was now too far away, the game had disappeared and many of the surface gold workings on the plateau had been worked out. By their failure to conserve their resources they had angered the most ancient spirits of the land.

Many of the people moved away and the stone capital city of Great Zimbabwe shrank to regional importance in the new Kingdom of Monomatapa. Later it retained only religious significance. The last Rozwi priest occupying the shrine on the hill was killed by a minor Karanga chief named Mugabe in the 1830s. Occasional rituals were still being performed there in the early years of the present century.

The carved soapstone bird motif, which represented the national ancestor spirits of Great Zimbabwe, was adopted as a national emblem by later European immigrants. But this was not as a tribute to 13 the forefathers of the indigenous builders, for the settlers clung tenaciously to the belief that the walls had been erected by white men like themselves. In their minds, the emblem linked them with the people they imagined had been there before the black men came, thus giving themselves the right of ancient tenure to the land that possessed them root and soul.

But such myths are little reassurance now to people who, although they would express it differently, feel suddenly that they no longer know the spirits of the land. Today the spirits of Great Zimbabwe and Malindidzimu are in dispute over their places in the pantheon of the new Zimbabwe of the future.

There is a nine-hole golf course now where, in the fields behind the hill, Mugabe drove off the defenders of the shrine almost a century and a half ago. Today, drumbeats summon the guests to meals at a nearby hotel, but there are racks for patrons' guns in the bar, and the manager dresses for dinner, with a sub-machine gun over his tuxedoed shoulder.

The old commerce in soapstone carvings is carried on by the curio shop at the site museum. On the floor a squadron of toy wooden aeroplanes made in the neighbouring tribal lands is lined up to take off on new trade routes.

And the raucous notes of the *n'anga's* kudu horn trumpet sound through the valley from where he is entertaining tourists in the replica Karanga village between the tea garden and the great Elliptical Enclosure.

The Kingdom of Monomatapa

Mupanje wekunze unodzivirira iri mukati
The outer ridge guards those inside
Shona proverb

Monomatapa seems today more like the name of a fabled kingdom than of a real one due to the fantasies of Ophir, Phoenicians, Solomon and Sheba woven by sixteenth century Portuguese and nineteenth century Victorians. Misled by imaginative Portuguese cartographers, early Dutch governors at the Cape of Good Hope dispatched expedition after expedition into the desert hinterland of the west coast in search of the legendary city of Vigiti Magna, and Davagul, capital of the golden empire of King Monomatapa. When they could not find them there, they began doubting whether they had ever existed.

But Monomatapa was a real kingdom. It was created out of the tradition of Great Zimbabwe some 600 years ago by a powerful Rozwi leader and, in its heyday, it included all of present-day Rhodesia and that part of Moçambique which lies between the Zambezi and Sabi rivers, the high mountains of Manicaland and the Indian Ocean. For half a millennium before Cecil John Rhodes arrived on the plateau, the Monomatapas and their successors, the Rozwi Mambos, were lords of the whole territory of what became Rhodesia.

At the height of its affluence, Great Zimbabwe was ruled by chiefs of the Rozwi clan, who originated in the Katanga region of Central Africa. The last of these people migrated southwards across the Zambezi in about 1335 under the leadership of NeMbire, whose lineage became the Mbire priesthood of Mwari.

But the ultimate destiny of this lineage lay in a different part of the country and Mambos from another Rozwi lineage would eventually seize power and rule most of the territory governed by the Mbire.

The eastern half of the central plateau, north from Great Zimbabwe to the edge of the escarpment overlooking the Zambezi, is mainly savanna woodland, in which large areas of msasa, mfuti and mnondo trees are interspersed with open areas of fine grazing for cattle and game. Therefore, when natural resources around Great Zimbabwe were exhausted early in the fifteenth century, Mutota, NeMbire's great-great-grandson, led his army northward, conquering an empire for himself and earning the praise-name Mwene Mutapa (Monomatapa), the Master Pillager, which became the hereditary title of his dynasty.

His son, Matope, made his capital in the northern province of the empire and installed his close relatives as governors of the newly-conquered eastern highland province of Manyika and other provinces in what is now Moçambique. The central province and old southern province, including Great Zimbabwe, he placed under his trusted friends, Togwa and Changa.

The Monomatapas were divine rulers who retained the allegiance of an extended trading empire because they alone could communicate with the spirits of their ancestors, the former kings. In times of drought and other natural crises, only they could ask the national lion spirits, the *mhondoro,* to intercede with Mwari on behalf of the people.

A fire, the source of every fire in the kingdom, burned at the royal court throughout the Monomatapa's reign. When he died, every fire in the kingdom was put out, and the provincial governors had to come and rekindle their fires from the fire of the new Monomatapa and then pass it on to the people.

At the royal court the Monomatapa's sovereign status was dramatised and enhanced by a host of court officials and praise-singers. Strict protocol required all seeking audience with him to throw themselves on the ground upon entering his presence, grovel at his feet and make their requests while lying on their sides and clapping their hands, their eyes respectfully averted. Here, too, the sons of provincial governors and other influential men were kept hostage to ensure the loyalty of their fathers. And in each of the provinces there was a token royal court where some of his wives lived permanently, creating the fiction that the Monomatapa had his home in every part of the kingdom.

It took a strong personality to carry it off. When Matope's son, Nyahuma, turned out to be a weakling, his father's old friends, Changa and Togwa, well aware that they controlled two thirds of the territory and the sources of most of the wealth of the kingdom, joined forces in 1490 and killed him.

Changa, the dominant conspirator, ruled the kingdom for only four years before the murdered Monomatapa's son avenged his father's death by killing him, but he became the founder of a new dynasty. His son

was able to hold on to the southern provinces, and his name, combined with the title *amir* given him by Arab traders, was perpetuated in the Changamire succession which ruled the greater part of the former Kingdom of Monomatapa for the next 300 years. A strip of territory along the Zambezi and down the coast was all the Monomatapas retained of their former domains.

When the Portuguese replaced the Arab and Swahili traders on the coast at Sofala in 1550, the ruling Changamire put a bar on their entering the gold producing area between Zimbabwe and the Matopos. This restriction was so rigidly enforced that, over a century later, captured Portuguese had to settle down and marry local women. For them there could be no hope of eventual release. Their captors knew that the moment they were out of the territory the secrets of the Rozwi confederacy would be known to the world.

The Rozwi were able to sell their gold at trade fairs in Monomatapa territory, without the Portuguese buyers discovering its source, and they prospered in their freedom from outside interference, while the Monomatapas, who no longer controlled the sources of wealth, were forced into a series of compromises with the Portuguese. They began by allowing Portuguese planters to settle along the Zambezi between Sena and Tete, then became reliant on them for military aid to maintain their authority over their subjects, and finally, in gratitude for assistance in settling a succession dispute, Monomatapa Mavura ceded his whole kingdom to the Portuguese crown in 1629 and became a Portuguese vassal. Thereafter the Portuguese enjoyed a free hand in his territory, but 60 years later, after a three-year war, Rozwi armies finally drove the Portuguese and the Monomatapa from their remaining footholds on the plateau.

Ripples from this war fought on the Zambezi were felt as far away as the Transvaal, south of the Limpopo, where today the royal clan of the Lovedu trace their descent from the old Monomatapas, and their Rain Queen is the most celebrated rain-maker in southern Africa, performing her rites with an amulet that was once the property of the kings themselves.

The man who after the war bore the title was left with no more authority than a local chief, and he had to live close to the Portuguese garrisons on the Zambezi for protection.

His forebears had brought powerful strangers into their country to settle their internal problems, forgetting that the outer ridge of a field is there to guard those inside – *mupanje wekunze unodzivirira iri mukati.*

Their descendants suffered for their indiscretion and the last of the Monomatapas, Chioko, was killed by these strangers in 1917.

Eastern Ramparts

Ushe imhute inoparara zuva rabuda
Chieftainship is fog; it vanishes at sunrise
Shona proverb

'There is a new green land in the country . . .' runs the jingle in a Rhodesian television commercial for fresh vegetables from Cashel Valley. It conjures up a picture of healthy greens being grown by carefree people in an idyllic setting under a smiling sun – the kind of environment in which, unconsciously, one expects one's vegetables to have started life, but also a subliminal reassurance that there may still be parts of the countryside that match the picture.

The nearby village of Melsetter, says the guidebook, is 'one of those beautiful, tranquil places to which many Rhodesians aim to retire'. It was written only a year or two ago. They haven't changed it, because they expect it to be that way again fairly soon.

There are five cars in the convoy on the 150 kilometre run from Umtali to Melsetter, which passes the entrance to the Cashel Valley. Light escort trucks, one in front and one behind, have five-man Police Anti-terrorist Unit crews, and each has a heavy belt-fed machine gun mounted on a spindle behind the cab. Two sub-machine gun barrels stick out on either side, and the crash-helmeted gunner, in harness behind the steel shield of the heavy Browning, traverses from side to side, scanning the steep, thickly-wooded slopes through his sights.

The little motorcade moves along at a steady 90 kilometres an hour, the drivers trying to maintain a constant 100-metre gap between themselves and the cars in front and behind. But they all bunch up on the long, slow inclines, when they feel vulnerable, and spread out on the fast descents. If someone lets a gap get too wide, those behind become edgy and mutter about the convoy splitting in two and breaking up.

The bush thins and the land flattens after a while, and the countryside is more open, with more grassland between the trees and more plain between the hills. It releases some of the tension. That an ambush party here would have a long way to flee to cover before the gunboat helicopter comes to mop up is an unspoken thought.

'It was about here they revved the convoy last time,' the driver tells the girl beside him. 'First you see little puffs of smoke in the grass, eight on either side, and you know they are shooting at you. Then, just when you think you are through, there are another six.'

The tension floods back. The girl peers more intently into the grass at the roadside.

Tribesmen hoeing their fields scarcely raise their heads as the convoy of heavily-armed white people sails through their fields. The occasional clusters of traditional thatched huts are deserted because tribespeople in border areas have been moved into new defended villages, to protect those who will not co-operate with the guerillas and to restrict those who will.

Further on, the driver points to a cultivated field beside a kopje. 'That's where Louw got slotted on his tractor last week,' he says. 'One of the last farmers still on his land around here . . .'

Once more the bush crowds in on higher, steeper slopes on both sides of the road. Three streams, three bridges, the middle one cracked by explosives, and the bunched convoy begins crawling up to Skyline.

'*Slagtersnek* (butcher's pass) we call it,' mutters the driver, leaning forward, rolling his eyes back to seek out the figure of a man with a rocket launcher who will one day appear on the heights.

'Through again,' breathes the girl, and they smile once more as the convoy gathers speed and spreads out along the descent.

The driver raises his hand and then hesitates. Three little black girls holding hands beside the road return vacant stares. 'Have you noticed that the piccanins no longer wave like they used to?' he asks.

'They're afraid,' says the girl.

Melsetter below is deep in the afternoon shadows of the hills. On the border, beyond the village and the pine forests, the white quartzite massif of the Chimanimani Mountains – thrust, folded and sheared against the unyielding Melsetter plain more than 1 000 million years ago – has a waxy lustre in the last of the direct sunlight.

Umtali, Cashel and Melsetter occupy valleys in a chain of high mountains that for centuries has been the 'outer ridge' protecting the peoples of the central plateau against invasion from the Moçambique coast.

These eastern ramparts had their origin during a

very ancient period of earth movement, in which the troughs of the great Central African lakes were depressed to below sea-level, while compensating forces raised other areas of the land surface high above their former levels. The eastern edge of the granite shield that underlies the central plateau of present-day Rhodesia was raised thousands of metres above sea-level by these forces, so that the whole plateau was tilted to slope down towards the west.

Since that time, many millions of years ago, ice and water have planed the midlands and corroded the northern and southern flanks into rolling hills. But in the eastern part of the plateau, erosion into the Zambezi and Sabi worked faster and cut deeper, all but severing the Eastern Highlands from the rest of the plateau and leaving only a narrow causeway of high ground along the watershed to connect them and the destinies of their inhabitants.

It is forever the wet season in the Highlands, where perennial maritime winds heap clouds on the windward slopes, trail mists through the valleys and deposit drizzle and heavy rain at all times of year. And the streams that channel all this water into the Odzi and Sabi, in the west, and the Honde, Pungwe and Gairezi, in the east, have carved out between them a rugged mountainland that has a climate and even a history of its own.

The highest peak, Inyangani, which rises to almost 2 600 metres in the north of this mountain chain, owes its name to a famous medicine man, an *n'anga,* who practised there early in the last century with such success that the whole district became known as Inyanga. But the story of human habitation there and throughout the Highlands goes back a lot further than that.

Stone artefacts and rock paintings disclose a long pre-historical period of occupancy before Ziwa people cultivated the red soil in the secluded grassland valleys on the western flank of Inyangani and the first black people on the plateau were settling in for their brief stay on the hill at Great Zimbabwe.

But in historical times, the story of the Highland peoples has to do chiefly with the rôle dictated by their geographical situation between the Rozwi rulers on the plateau and the gold-hungry Portuguese on the coast. They occupied the 'outer ridge' of the Rozwi state, and so were not among those inside who were protected by it. Evidence of their insecurity may be seen to this day in their refuges on the forested uplands and undulating downs at Inyanga, where the remains of their stone forts, walled agricultural terraces, irrigation furrows and stone-lined pits are scattered over a wide area.

Manyika, as the Highlands were then called, was a province of the Kingdom of Monomatapa, but it had become virtually independent by the end of the sixteenth century. This fledgling independence, however, was held in low regard in the Portuguese trading settlements on the lower Zambezi, where Manyika was coveted for its gold mines and the ingress it gave to the Rozwi heartland.

Today, Manyika tribesmen still have a saying: *MaZungu manyoka/haatani kuumbuka* – 'the Portuguese are like inflamed bowels, they quickly change'. It is a legacy of the early seventeenth century, when the Portuguese came into the Highlands and disrupted local politics, taking first one side then the other, as it suited them, in disputes between chiefs. In the 1630s they killed the ruling Chicanga of Manyika, set up their own nominee on his throne and established permanent trade fairs in several places.

The Rozwi on the plateau became increasingly concerned when they saw that the 'outer ridge' of their domain was being breached by a growing stream of traders and prospectors, and in 1690 they sent an army to extinguish Portuguese influence in the Highlands. Although the Rozwi had also benefited from the trade, another three decades passed before they permitted the Portuguese to re-open the fairs near present-day Umtali, the Vumba and at Vila de Manica in what is now Moçambique. Here, on the strict understanding that they were not themselves to take part in mining or attempt to gain political control, they were allowed to trade liquor, cloth, beads, gunpowder and firearms for ivory, wax, rock crystal, skins and the best gold that was available in the eighteenth century.

The Highlands remained in the balance struck between Portuguese trade and Rozwi power until the 1830s when new black invaders, the Ngoni who came from the vicinity of present-day Swaziland, stormed up through southern Moçambique, conquered the Rozwi on the plateau, overran settlements on the Highlands and sacked the Manyika fairs.

Taking advantage of the unsettled state of the country, Portuguese fortune-hunters, adventurers and desperados flooded into the Highlands, among them the notorious Manuel Antonio de Sousa, who rode through Manyika with a private army and his great war drum, Chiuzingu, over which a captive's throat was ceremonially slit before the bloody hide was beaten to summon a defeated tribe to do him homage.

Portuguese influence in this region depended almost entirely upon the presence of such wandering gangs of bandits. To give the Portuguese government a stronger claim to the territory, the authorities in Lisbon appointed de Sousa *capitao-mor* of Manyika. Driving a hard bargain for desperately needed military aid, de Sousa pressured Mutasa, King of Manyika, into recognising him as overlord, and he was ritually presented with earth from the spirit medium's hut to symbolise the transfer of sovereignty over the land.

Aware that British interests had designs on the country, de Sousa was in 1888 instrumental in launching a company in Lisbon to establish formal Portuguese control over the goldfields of the central plateau as well as Manyika. But by the time he tried to put this into effect the British had already occupied the plateau, and the Eastern Highlands offered them their only prospect of railway access to the sea. And so, when de Sousa returned to Mutasa's kraal for confirmation of his overlordship, the British South Africa Police were there to arrest him and send him overland as a prisoner to Cape Town. The legality of the move is questionable, but with de Sousa out of the way and no one else to assert Portuguese claims, old Manyika became the province of Manicaland in the new Rhodesia.

Umtali, name of the chief centre in Manicaland, means 'metal' and probably refers to gold, but no gold has ever been mined where the city is today. The explanation is that the gold mine is still where it was 90 years ago, while Umtali has moved – twice. It began 18 kilometres north of where it is now as a police post, Fort Umtali, at the gold workings in the Penhalonga Valley. It moved first when an enterprising prospector pegged the site of the fort as his claim and a second time a few years later when it was found that the new railway line to Beira would bypass the town.

Flanked by massive granite mountains, it lies in a broad valley which gives natural access from the plateau to the coastlands of Moçambique. But today there is a political barrier across the valley. The frontier is closed. And after a mortar bomb landed in the main street, the military bulldozed a broad scar through the hills along the border, erected security fences on either side of it and salted it with landmines. But in the springtime the streets are still lilac-blue with jacaranda blossom and the scarlet flamboyants still blaze through into summer. And despite its cathedral, Umtali remains less a city than a provincial town, strung out in low profile on either side of a long tarred street.

The old colonial-style Cecil Hotel building has been taken over as command headquarters, and the mysterious ticking heard late at night from the air-conditioned upper floors of the new hotel is the sound of the teleprinter next door punching the daily report through to Combined Operations headquarters in Salisbury.

Old soldiers in panama hats, blazers and white flannels meet in the afternoon for bowls and a noggin at the Shellhole. Young railwaymen, who are part-time soldiers, bend over snooker tables at the mess.

A row of mine-proofed Landrovers with their front wheels blown off await repair in a field of orange flowers. On outlying private estates, mansions in exotic gardens landscaped with ponds, streams and waterfalls, recall a more sedate interlude which also once seemed as if it would last forever.

From the summit of the Vumba, some 30 kilometres south-east of Umtali, there are glimpses of emerald hills in Moçambique through partings in the perpetual mists that gave the mountain its name. In the Bunga forest on the slopes, your feet sink ankle deep in the leafmould and, even on the hottest days, the air is cool and moist and humus-scented.

An every-day baker's delivery van passes on its leisurely rounds, and for a moment the mine-proofing and safety harness in the Landrover seem like the trappings of paranoia.

The façade of the Leopard Rock Hotel is scarred from the last time guerillas sprayed it with bullets and rocket fire, but in the garden below, the headwaiter, in white smock and crimson sash and tarbush, is pruning the rose bushes.

At Melsetter, the garage people are getting ready to leave with the convoy in the morning – for good, or until things get better. They have had enough of the tension. They are moving to somewhere safer, like Umtali.

'Don't go,' people say, but no one says anything bitter, like 'chicken run' or 'taking the yellow route', because they all know that they may come to this point too.

The gloom of the pine plantations seems to have seeped into the village that was founded with such optimism by the pioneers who trekked here from the Orange Free State less than 90 years ago.

The hotel has an air of desolation. A small group of timber company employees and a few wives are making a sundowner last in the cocktail bar. The wives talk about their fuchsias and inviting a guest speaker from Salisbury to the next meeting of their horticultural club. The men discuss the things that men discuss all over the country in these times. They believe they are marked men, known by name to the guerillas, who may at any time decide to make an example of any one of them.

There is bravado, fatalism, in their laughter, and the stories they relate are about their own close shaves and narrow escapes. But by the time the Chimanimani Mountains through the lounge window have changed their colour to dark grey the only people still in the bar are men wearing the uniform of a private army engaged to patrol the plantations and tea and coffee estates on the border.

At supper they occupy a bright corner in the dimly lit dining-room, swopping anecdotes about their escapades in other little wars – Mau Mau, the Congo, Biafra – over the best red wine in the house.

The hotel stands in floodlit surroundings, but inside there are pools of darkness.

Conquest of the Plateau

My strongest belief is in power . . . But what is the end of power? So often desert sand or ruins. But there is a force, a power and a vitality that drives one on, and one cannot evade it if one would. Cecil John Rhodes

Until the second quarter of the nineteenth century all migrants and invaders who entered the plateau had come from the north. But over the next 70 years the people of this region were overwhelmed by three separate waves of conquerors who swept into the country from the south: the Ngoni, who terminated 300 years of Rozwi rule and went away; the Ndebele, who occupied the south-western end of the plateau and forced Shona tribes over a wide area to pay them tribute; the British, who took possession of the whole land and made it Rhodesia.

A poignant final scene on a hilltop north-east of present-day Bulawayo brought down the curtain on the Rozwi state in the 1830s. Fleeing before Ngoni invaders, the last Mambo and his people were finally besieged on the hill that would afterwards be called Taba zi ka Mambo in commemoration of the event. From the heights they threw down beads, skins, hoes and everything they had of value and promised the invaders cattle and sheep if they would leave them in peace, but their attackers would not desist.

Next day the Mambo appeared with his councillors on an overhanging rock and called on the Ngoni to hear his latest peace offer. Then, as they waited for his words, he hurled himself from the ledge and fell 30 metres to his death at their feet. Such was the shock that his people were able to slip away that night, and the following day the invaders moved on, leaving his mangled corpse where it had fallen, as food for the hyaena, the jackal and the vulture.

The loose confederation of chiefdoms under the Rozwi had been no match for the Ngoni who, although they had themselves been obliged to flee from Shaka's superior forces in the south, had nevertheless been tempered in the same flame as the militaristic Zulus.

19

But, apart from a division under Soshangane, which established itself east of the Sabi and became the forefathers of the Shangaan living in the south-east lowveld today, the Ngoni cut their way northward like a broad-bladed stabbing assegai to the territories of modern Zambia, Malawi and Tanzania, sacking Zimbabwe and the Rozwi centres at Khami and Dhlo Dhlo as they passed through.

But although the great Rozwi dynasties' power was smashed, leaving the Shona vulnerable to the next wave of invaders, their religious system has been preserved to this day as a rallying point for wider Shona nationalism. Many still regard the Rozwi as the Elect of Mwari, and chiefdoms formerly in the confederation observe the tradition that the installation of a new chief must have Rozwi approval and confirmation.

Shona is not a name which these people gave to themselves. Meaning 'those who are lost', it was bestowed on the Karanga by the conquering Ndebele and afterwards extended by European administrators to all groups speaking dialects of the same language: Karanga, Zezuru, Manyika, Korekore, Rozwi, Ndau and Kalanga.

They were cultivators more than cattle herders and lived in small scattered villages that were at the mercy of the compact military machine brought into the country by Mzilikazi in the wake of the Ngoni.

Mzilikazi's Ndebele, or 'people of the long shields', had also fled originally from the wrath of Shaka, whose sovereignty their leader had refused to accept. But they had left a trail of blood across the South African interior and forged themselves into a powerful nation before eventually being driven northward out of the Transvaal by the Boers. Local resistance on the plateau was easily overcome, and they built their kraals in the south-west of the country in what had been the major Rozwi area of settlement.

Their way of life differed markedly from that of the Shona. Husbandry and crop raising satisfied only part of their needs; raiding other peoples for cattle, food and men supplied the rest. Their social cement was not their occupation of a common territory but their common membership of a highly disciplined military system in which the king was supreme commander and held autocratic power of life and death over his subjects. They lived concentrated within an 80 kilometre radius of the royal kraal from where raiding parties were dispatched among the dispersed Shona. It was a way of life conditioned by circumstance. Had they lived differently, they would not have survived their formative years south of the Limpopo.

Many Shona living in the Ndebele area of settlement were absorbed into the military system as a lower caste, others adopted the language of the conquerors. Outside the circle were Shona who had been subdued by raids but were left to continue their own internal political and religious lives, provided they paid regular tribute to the Ndebele king. At the time when Europeans entered the country in force in 1890 Ndebele impis were still raiding west of present-day Salisbury and around Great Zimbabwe, but east of the Sabi and in the northern provinces of the old Kingdom of Monomatapa they had not yet set foot.

Europeans were not welcomed by the Ndebele. Mzilikazi saw clearly that the presence of white men in his territory would ultimately bring it within a powerful sphere of foreign interest. But in 1859 he was persuaded to make an exception in the case of his old friend, the missionary Robert Moffat, and allowed him to establish a mission station under his son, John Moffat, although he made sure it gained no influence among his people. Then, shortly before his death nine years later, he permitted some hunters to shoot elephant in his domain, and the discovery of ancient gold workings by one of them, Henry Hartley, aroused interest in the 'far north' among the fortune-hunters who were gathering like flies at the Cape.

When Lobengula succeeded his father as king he was besieged by concession-seekers. A few traders were admitted and permission was given for a few small groups of Boer and Griqua hunters to make limited expeditions into his territory. Frederick Courteney Selous, who was to become the most famous of the white hunters, was given freedom to travel and hunt wherever he so wished, because, at 20, Lobengula thought him too young to achieve anything. One gold concession was granted at Tati, in what is today Botswana, and another was obtained by the artist-explorer Thomas Baines. But for the rest, the men who arrived with the glint of gold in their eyes either gave up and returned home when their funds ran out or lingered in the growing community of prospectors and adventurers petitioning for Lobengula's favour at Bulawayo, his royal kraal.

For Lobengula, however, the writing was already on the wall. The European 'Scramble for Africa' – which seems today to have belonged to a remote age, although it in fact took place almost within living memory – had begun and would soon develop into the 'Scramble for Matabeleland'. Portuguese, Germans, Dutch, Belgians and Transvaal Republicans were all casting lustful glances at the land that lay north of the Limpopo. In the years that followed, Lobengula would admit that he felt like a fly waiting for the dart of a chameleon's tongue.

The chameleon took the form of Cecil John Rhodes, an Englishman in his mid-thirties who had already made his fortune on the Kimberley diamond fields and had thus acquired financial and political influence in both southern Africa and Britain. He so embodied the entrepreneurial imperialist spirit of his age that he became a caricature of it. He was not in his enterprises merely for the money. His dreams were visions of a railway system spanning Africa from the Cape to Cairo, all of it built through territory coloured pink on the map to denote British possession.

Lobengula was a shrewd diplomat, but he had few options and the trend of world events was against him. The land which he believed was his by right of conquest, Rhodes now plotted to take from him, by stealth if possible, or by force if necessary. When in 1887 Rhodes received reports from his spies at Bulawayo that Lobengula was allowing a large number of Transvaal farmers to hunt in his territory, he sensed a prelude to Boer settlement north of the Limpopo and decided to act.

Treaties with African sovereigns were sought during the 'Scramble' period not for any accord they might promote between African and European but because they furnished the European with a basis in international law for pre-empting other interested parties. Therefore, when the following year John Moffat obtained for Rhodes a treaty in which Lobengula promised not to enter into any agreement with another power without British approval, its implications were far wider than its negative purport suggested. Its effect was to bring Matabeleland into the British sphere of influence and warn off other European competitors.

Later the same year Rhodes acquired through a business partner, Charles Rudd, the so-called Rudd Concession, in which Lobengula granted the 'complete and exclusive' right to all minerals in his 'kingdom, principalities and domains, together with full power to do all things that they may deem necessary to win and procure same . . .'

Lobengula, however, had agreed to the Concession on verbal undertakings by Rudd that it would protect the Ndebele from further European pressure and that only ten Europeans would enter his territory to work the mines. Furthermore, it was agreed that these men would be under Ndebele law and liable for military service should Lobengula be attacked. But none of these solemn undertakings was written into the text of the Concession, and they were soon forgotten by the white men. They were not mentioned when the British South Africa Company was formed in London to work the Concession, nor when it received a charter from

the British Crown in October 1899 authorising it to proceed.

When Lobengula caught the scent of what was in the air he tried to repudiate the Concession and found reasons for postponing the entry of Company men into his territory. But although the Concession included no right to land, it did confer the right of access to its minerals and therefore of occupation. The deliberate fiction was concocted that all Mashonaland fell within Lobengula's domain and was thus included in the Concession. And on these 'legal' foundations the occupation of Mashonaland was planned.

Rhodes reasoned that this should be done by a route that skirted to the east of Matabeleland proper: if Lobengula left them alone he would be seen to tacitly condone the move; if he attacked them Rhodes would have a pretext for destroying him. Lobengula saw that he was doomed if he tried to fight and so allowed the Pioneer Column to pass.

The 200 hand-picked Pioneers, accompanied by about 400 newly-recruited British South Africa Company Police, set off on July 11, 1890 from Fort Tuli on their 700 kilometre march into Mashonaland, guided by the self-same Selous whose hunting prowess had so exceeded all Lobengula's expectations.

Where they climbed from the lowveld to the plateau they built and garrisoned Fort Victoria at the head of the pass. Fort Charter was likewise established on the headwaters of the Sabi, and on September 13 the flag was raised on the empty plain at Harare, where they built Fort Salisbury, which was to become the capital city of modern Rhodesia.

Three weeks later the Column was disbanded and each of its members was encouraged to select a 1 210 hectare farm and stake 15 gold claims for himself. An armed party, despatched to secure Manicaland, had to be recalled after they set out on their own initiative to conquer an outlet to the sea and capture the port of Beira. An aggressive policy towards the Portuguese resulted the following year in the drawing of Rhodesia's eastern boundary. Meanwhile, moves were undertaken in the north and west to completely surround Matabeleland with British territory.

In vain Lobengula attempted to play rival European interests off against one another by granting the Lippert Concession which gave the Germans land rights throughout his domain. But Lobengula was an innocent in the ways of European business and so played instead into the hands of Rhodes, who simply bought the concession from Lippert and so obtained a form of title to the land in addition to the one he already had to its mineral wealth.

However, the showdown with Lobengula had to 21

come. He was under constant pressure from his young warriors to drive the Europeans out of the country, while the white settlers, who felt threatened by the Ndebele, clamoured for a reckoning.

A pretext presented itself in October 1893 when an Ndebele impi made a punitive raid on Shona in the Fort Victoria area who had paid a fine imposed by the Company with cattle that belonged nominally to Lobengula. The Company claimed that, as the Shona were living under its protection, it was obliged to take action against the Ndebele king. Armed columns of irregulars, with promises of 30 gold claims and 2 420 hectares of farmland for every man at the end of the campaign, closed in on Lobengula from Salisbury, Fort Victoria and Tuli. In two sharp engagements the rapid-firing Maxim guns did great slaughter among the Ndebele, and on November 4 the Europeans occupied the smouldering ruins of the royal kraal at Bulawayo, which Lobengula had put to the torch before fleeing northwards.

A force was despatched immediately in pursuit of the king. Lobengula sent messages of peace and a bag of gold sovereigns as a token of his pacific wishes, but the gold was appropriated by some troopers and the messages were not relayed to the commanding officer. Then, on the Shangani River they received reports that Lobengula was near by on the opposite bank and, although it was already late in the day, a reconnaissance patrol under Major Allan Wilson was sent across. Cut off from the main force during the night by the rising waters of the Shangani, Wilson and his 34 men found themselves next morning grouped around an ant-hill in a mopane forest and surrounded by 3 000 Ndebele warriors.

It was the sort of stuff that legends are made of, the warp into which the bright threads of patriotism are woven. Without the Maxims that had given them the edge in previous battles and with no hope of mercy or relief, they could only fight to the last man. This is not the place to raise the old spectres of military incompetence and disobeyed orders or to examine the embellishments that the men sang *God Save the Queen* before they died and that the fight they put up was so fierce that it discouraged the Ndebele from continuing the war. In the legend the touches of heightened colour were accepted as part of the reality and earned the men a place beside Rhodes in the Rhodesian pantheon on the hill in the Matopos that is called Malindidzimu. A new country needs its heroes; new people in an old land need their protectors in the spirit world.

Several weeks after the pursuit was abandoned at the Shangani River, news came to Bulawayo that Lobengula had died somewhere in the north. His young sons were spirited off to the Cape to be educated so that there would be no claimants to the Ndebele throne. And to his collection of dubious titles to the land Rhodes was now able to add the right of conquest.

The extension of Company rule to Matabeleland brought a boom in prospecting, mining, farming and speculation; within two years Bulawayo, with 3 000 Europeans, had become the largest settlement in the country. The old Pioneer Road through Fort Victoria declined in importance and the new coach road from Tuli through Bulawayo and Gwelo to Salisbury became the major highway. Still on the crest of the commercial wave in 1895, the country of the Monomatapas and the Rozwi Mambos was officially renamed Rhodesia.

The wave broke a year later when first the Ndebele and then the Shona came out in armed rebellion against the government imposed on them by the Company.

Many reasons have been put forward for the rebellions including drought, locusts, rinderpest and east coast fever, but there is perhaps no better explanation than the self-deception of the settlers themselves. They believed that the Ndebele, whose social structure enshrined the military principle, had now meekly accepted a labouring rôle. Indeed, they believed the missionaries who, frustrated by their 30-year failure to make a single convert, thought that the Ndebele had only been waiting for the overthrow of Lobengula's tyranny to embrace the benefits of Christianity and civilization. They believed that the Shona welcomed their deliverance from the Ndebele yoke and were happy to pay for it in taxes and forced labour. They thought it of no consequence to the grateful Shona that their gold trade with the coast should be summarily suspended and that in place of Portuguese trade goods they should now pay more for goods of British manufacture. It did not occur to them that the Shona might resent the distribution of tribal land to settlers as farms from which they would henceforth be excluded in other than a menial capacity. Dazzled by the brilliance of the torch of civilization they carried to the central plateau, the settlers did not see that other peoples were attached to their own ways of life.

Inevitably, the rebellions were suppressed. In the name of the 'justice, freedom and commerce' proclaimed by the Company, the conquest of the plateau was complete. But power does not remain in the same hands forever, and, as the Shona say: 'the axe forgets but the log does not' – *Chinokanganwa idemo/chitsiga hachikanganwe.*

Sunshine and Storm

Chinozipa chinoregwa/zamu ramai takarirega
Whatever is delicious is to be left since we
gave up our mother's breast *Shona proverb*

The land which the white Pioneers occupied in 1890 and finally conquered seven years later was a land of rich and varied potential, but the fullness of its promise was to be unfolded only gradually by the steady advance of technology and the accumulative pressures of necessity.

The ancient schists bearing the veins of gold that attracted the first European settlers to this land also contained vast deposits of asbestos, chrome, copper, iron ores, iron pyrites, limestone, lithium and nickel and a host of other minerals that achieved significance only after innovations in distant parts of the world created uses for them. Huge reserves of chrome and asbestos also lay untouched in the unique sequence of igneous rocks called the Great Dyke, which cuts a swathe four to 11 kilometres broad across the plateau for over 500 kilometres from northern Mashonaland to the vicinity of present-day Gwanda in the south. At Wankie, in the north-west, the seemingly unlimited energy source of one of the largest high-grade coal deposits on earth waited to be harnessed.

By fortunate coincidence, the areas to which gold drew the first settlers were those which had not only plenty of sunshine and comfortable humidity levels but also the soils and rainfall most conducive to agriculture. Rhodesia is generally a dry country with poor soils, and only in the Eastern Highlands is the rainfall consistently high. Here the cool rugged hills that contort the land surface favour tree plantations, deciduous fruit orchards and estate crops such as coffee and tea, while the good growth of grass can support intensive livestock production.

To the west of the Highlands, the whole of central and most of north-east Mashonaland receives moderate and dependable rains which favour intensive crop and livestock farming. But further west, progressively poorer soils and lower, less-consistent rainfall support mixed farming in which livestock tends to predominate as conditions deteriorate. At the western end of the plateau and in the southern middleveld, the long dry spells discourage any but the most drought-resistant crops and those breeds of livestock that can be sustained in large measure by natural grazing.

The Zambezi basin and the Limpopo and Sabi lowveld were of no agricultural value before the conquest of the tsetse fly. Only then were they opened up for extensive livestock production based entirely on natural grazing and, more recently, major irrigation projects have made the south-eastern lowveld 'bloom'.

These developments, however, lay well into the future. The early settlers expected no more from their limited agriculture than the supply of their own food. Indeed, for several years in the beginning they obtained many of their immediate food requirements from the local population. The Shona had always been essentially cultivators rather than pastoralists and the new crop varieties that found their way into the area over the centuries through the Zambezi Valley had enabled them to develop a complex agriculture. The first settlers found the tribesmen cultivating maize, poko corn, sorghum, millet, rice, peanuts, five sorts of bean, egg fruit, peas, cabbages, tomatoes, pumpkins, water-melons, cucumbers, sweet potatoes, chillies, tobacco, bananas and lemons – and 'all these grown to perfection'.

Despite the natural resources available to evolve a broadly based economy with a high degree of self-sufficiency, Rhodesia developed a typically 'colonial' economy that depended mainly on the export of primary produce and the import of large quantities of manufactured goods.

The economic growth of modern Rhodesia was supported by the steel framework of the railway system constructed in the early years. By mid-1897 Bulawayo was connected to the Cape by a new railway line running through what was then Bechuanaland; the following year a line from the Moçambique port of Beira reached Umtali on the eastern border. It took another year to link Salisbury and Umtali and a further three years to bridge the gap between Salisbury and Bulawayo. A line laid northwards from Bulawayo reached the Wankie coalfields in 1903 and crossed the Zambezi at Victoria Falls a year later. Branch lines brought the important mines and mining areas into the system and connected them to the country's major domestic energy source on one hand and external markets on the other.

For the first decade of this century all other econo- 23

mic activities were subsidiary to mining and right up to the end of the 1930s Rhodesia remained primarily a mining country, with gold as its major product and export.

The vague notion that somewhere north of the Limpopo, goldfields the size of a 'Second Witwatersrand' awaited discovery, encouraged the settlers to register some 160 000 gold claims by 1898. But the black miners who for centuries past had mined the gold of the plateau had in fact worked out all the more easily accessible deposits down to water level. Now only the big producers could bear the high costs of reaching the less accessible deposits and processing the poorer grade ores which led rapidly to the concentration of the industry in their hands.

Peak production of 830 000 ounces was achieved in 1940 and thereafter gold production declined due to rising costs and static market prices. By this time, however, tobacco was well on its way to replacing gold as both main product and chief export. In 1948 the ascendancy of agriculture over mining was established when tobacco overtook gold as chief export. In the mining sphere gold was similarly losing ground; the increasing exploitation and value of other minerals led to asbestos ousting gold as chief mineral by 1952.

The settlers' earliest experiments with tobacco cultivation had been in the western part of the country with the coarser, sun-dried varieties, but in 1904 a first crop of flue-cured Virginia leaf had been so successful that the cultivation of this variety shifted to the east, where conditions were ideal. By 1922 annual production had topped 1,5 million kilos and over the next five years it increased sixfold. By the end of the 1930s some 30 million kilos were being exported every year.

Up until the Second World War, therefore, the essentially 'colonial' pattern of the Rhodesian economy remained largely unchanged. But this was altered when the war cut off external supplies of manufactured goods and made the country more dependent on local production. Manufacturing, which until then had been ancillary to mineral and agricultural production, began occupying a significant position of its own. By 1964 it was responsible for 18,5 percent of the Gross Domestic Product and was on the verge of overtaking agriculture, while mining lagged far behind at only six percent. Manufacturing was also providing 40 percent of exports against 33,3 percent from tobacco and 23 percent from all mineral production.

The political events which resulted in the country's Unilateral Declaration of Independence (UDI) from Britain in 1965, and the imposition as a result of two-way trade sanctions, confronted the economy with new challenges. Vital imports were cut off, while the exports on which the country relied for foreign exchange could no longer be sold unless the country of origin was heavily disguised.

The initial effect on manufacturing was that it slipped back to second place behind agriculture as the largest single contributor to the national income. One third of the gross· manufacturing output had been exported in 1965. Now, with the sudden loss of a substantial part of its external market, industry was left with spare capacity with which to supply a domestic market clamouring for a wide range of products that had previously been imported. In addition, methods had to be devised for recycling imported raw materials, and for the further processing of products that had previously been exported in their raw or crude state, thereby concealing their origin more effectively. Industry had also to gear itself to satisfy the demand for a large number of intermediate products. Where, for instance, the country had formerly exported cotton, imported cloth and manufactured clothing, a new textile industry now emerged to fill the gap between the raw material and the final product. At the same time, export markets had to be found and sustained under conditions of the greatest secrecy.

Manufacturing displayed great versatility in meeting these challenges, chiefly through the ingenuity of small-scale producers. The variety of locally manufactured commodities rose from little more than 1 000 to slightly less than 4 000 in four years. Within a few years manufacturing had once again risen to pre-eminence and by 1974 it was contributing more to the national income than agriculture and mining combined.

Agriculture faced similar challenges. Tobacco, its mainstay, had been exported to over 30 countries in 1965 and had accounted for 44 percent of the total agricultural product. As its distinctive quality made it easy to detect on overseas markets, farmers were forced to diversify and aimed at raising output, with self-sufficiency in all food products as their objective.

In large measure this was made possible by subsidies, inducements, applied agricultural research, the breeding of new strains that were better suited to local conditions, and a policy of large-scale dam building for irrigation, which began in the years before UDI and was continued and expanded afterwards. The availability of water for irrigation created opportunities for introducing winter crops on land that had previously lain fallow during the dry season. It extended the growing season in areas where it was sometimes too short for crops to mature fully and helped standing crops over mid-season dry spells which would otherwise have spoilt or ruined them.

The success with which agriculture has implemented the double objectives of diversification and self-sufficiency is mirrored in the production figures. Since UDI cattle, dairy produce and sugar output have doubled, tea has trebled, peanut production has quadrupled. Maize output has increased sixfold, cotton tenfold, wheat 26 times, soya beans 60 times, while tobacco production has fallen by a quarter.

In the mining sector, Government assistance and improved prices encouraged the exploitation of some 50 different minerals. But asbestos, the chief mineral, presented a problem: it was of such high quality with fibres of such exceptional length that it could not be masqueraded as originating in any other country. It became necessary to break up the fibres into shorter lengths and deliberately debase the product in order to sell it on world markets. How similar problems have been overcome in the case of chrome and other minerals is a closely guarded secret.

Since the short period of post-UDI reorientation the real output of manufacturing, agriculture and mining taken together has increased at an average annual rate of between eight and nine percent.

While the internal responses to sanctions have broadened, strengthened and integrated the economic base of the country, the Rhodesian economy has suffered greatly in other ways particularly in the cost in manpower and materials of fighting a protracted bush war of mounting intensity. Economists question whether reliance on the domestic market can sustain growth indefinitely or whether expansion will reach a ceiling beyond which it will not be able to go without the stimulus of foreign investment and wider markets.

The forgotten factor in the economic equation is that for the 80-odd years of its existence Rhodesia has had not one economy but two operating side-by-side: the white-dominated cash economy and the subsistence economy of the vast black majority of its people.

When the pioneers first occupied the plateau, the black population was only about half a million and the sufficiency of land on which they could continue their traditional way of life was such that they could only be induced to enter the cash economy as labourers on the settlers' mines and farms by coercive means like taxes and fines. But today the total population of the country is in the vicinity of seven million, of whom 95 percent are black. Of this black population some two million are more or less equally divided between the urban areas and the white-owned farms, while about five million are regarded as residents of the designated tribal areas.

These so-called Tribal Trust Lands, which today spread over half the country, are generally the poorer agricultural lands, which have lighter soils, higher temperatures and lower rainfalls than the white farming areas. Two-thirds of this land is so poor that it scarcely provides subsistence for the people living on it. Families on the Tribal Trust Lands are increasingly dependent for cash subsidies on workers in the towns and on the white farms. The tribal areas, however, do feed and accommodate at the subsistence level a large percentage of the black population, for whom industry has not yet grown sufficiently to provide employment. In this regard the achievements of industry have been subsidised by the tribal economy.

Explosive population growth in recent years has intensified pressure on tribal land to the point where average population density is 30 to the square kilometre. Although attempts to alleviate this situation with large development projects have been impressive, the crux remains that there are too many people on the land and industrial growth has not been able to keep pace with population growth.

The old colonial attitudes, in which black people were regarded as a nation apart, have persisted through to the present. It is nevertheless true that, although the quality of black labour was regularly disparaged, the triumphs of white capital would have been impossible without it. The 'winds of change' that howled through Africa also gusted over the Rhodesian plateau. Dissatisfied with their share in the rewards of industry, the black people began seeing the solution to their problems in the conquest of the political kingdom, and their discontent was articulated in a call for political change that grew ever more strident.

In lunch-hour Salisbury, black city workers doze and play games of Arabian origin in the leafy shade on Cecil Square, where in 1890 the Pioneers raised the Union Jack and fired a 21-gun salute one fine September morning to mark the addition of yet another land to the British Empire.

After almost 90 years, the city that grew up around the site still retains traces of an English heritage. In the suburbs, orderly English-style gardens, with manicured lawns, tidy flower-beds, lavender-scented shrubberies and ornamental trees, are secluded behind neatly-trimmed hedges of pink and red hibiscus. Along the broad streets leading to the city centre, the quaint British custom of transplanting the flora of their far-flung colonial possessions lingers in the avenues of flowering lilac jacaranda, red flamboyant, white bauhinia, orange-trumpeted spathodeas and heavy-headed yellow cassias.

Beyond the suburbs lie the industrial areas and the encircling black townships teeming with the crowds of 25 the market-place and the bus depots, where more functional gardens sprout vegetables and wrecked car bodies, and where traditional herbalists in business suits deal in ancient remedies.

But the city centre is a pleasing blend of Europe and Africa, where the low buildings between the tall ones open windows to sun and sky and there is none of the grime of English manufacturing towns. And since the colour bar was lifted, black and white mingle in sidewalk cafés and around tables in paved malls, and only the names of the thoroughfares, which perpetuate the memory of colonial heroes, seem to be vaguely out of joint with the times.

Salisbury is the home of more than half the entire white population of Rhodesia but the black residents outnumber them three to one. Harare, once the name of the area, is now the name of one of the townships, but black leaders, who have no wish to remember the long-dead British prime minister, Lord Salisbury, say that someday soon the whole city will be Harare.

The supermarkets are crammed with foods produced locally, from cheese and jam to whiskey and freshly-caught trout. Here one is less conscious of the bush war than one is in the smaller towns. People do not walk about the streets armed. At the entrances to shops, hotels and office buildings hand luggage is opened for the scrutiny of security guards as a matter of course, and periodically police with whistles cordon off a section of street to check that no one is carrying a bomb. Salisbury seems to be suspended between two worlds, between Jameson Avenue and Harare.

The Power and the Glory

Mvura bvongodzeki ndiyo garani
Troubled water becomes peaceful *Shona proverb*

The mighty Zambezi River flows more than 3 000 kilometres from its source on the border between Angola and Zambia to its mouth on the Moçambique coast. For some 800 kilometres of its middle course, from where it is joined by the Chobe River in the west to its confluence with the Luangwa in the east, it forms Rhodesia's northern border with Zambia.

East of its junction with the Chobe, the Zambezi flows over a bed of basaltic lava that was spread hundreds of metres thick over the surrounding countryside many millions of years ago. The river flows over this basalt for about 60 kilometres until suddenly it plunges in a two-kilometre wide curtain of water more than 100 metres into a gorge carved by the torrent out of a huge fault in the rock. This gorge of the famed Victoria Falls is only the most recent in a zig-zag series of high-sided faults that through the ages were incised downstream in similar fashion and each in its time was the chasm into which the great waterfall thundered as the Zambezi cut its way back gorge by gorge through the faults.

From below the gorges where the river enters the Gwembe trough to where the dam wall now stands the old riverbed lies deep beneath the surface of one of the largest man-made lakes in the world, 280 kilometres long, 42 kilometres across at its widest and covering an area of about 5 200 square kilometres.

Some 1 000 years ago the Gwembe trough was inhabited by the ancestors of the present Tonga tribe, whose origins are uncertain. These people were unable to keep cattle, as the valley was infested with tsetse fly, but they were expert fishermen, cultivated the river banks, hunted and kept some smallstock.

Throughout the known period of their history, the Tonga have fared badly at the hands of other peoples with whom they came into contact. They were subdued so vigorously by the first Monomatapa that they spoke of his armies as 'locusts' – *Korekore* – a name by which a neighbouring Shona tribe is known to this day. In the last century they were severely mauled, first by the Kololo, who had fled before the Ndebele to this region, and afterwards by the Ndebele themselves. Towards the end of the century the white hunter, Selous, reported seeing only old women in this area, as all the younger ones had been carried off into slavery.

The Tonga, who depended on the river for much of their livelihood, believe that its moods and rhythms are controlled by a river spirit named Nyaminyami.

Deep below the surface of Lake Kariba today is a dark rock that the Tonga called Ka-riwa. The name means 'little trap' but it is also another name for Nyaminyami. So potent was the symbolism of this rock that the Tonga spoke of it as if it *was* Nyaminyami. It was a symbolism that the builders of the wall that held back the Zambezi came to share. Nyaminyami became a metaphor for their efforts to come to terms with the power of the river.

Lake Kariba was created to operate a hydro-electric plant for supplying the territories on either side of the gorge with power – the power without which the post-UDI industrial development of Rhodesia would have been impossible.

From the outset, the project had to be scheduled to fit in with the seasonal moods of the river. The timetable called for the dam wall to be completed, the dam filled and the generators delivering electricity within four years of the project being officially approved. It was therefore crucial that the engineers start work at the beginning of the dry season.

The elephants who today gather in growing numbers along the shoreline are in a sense enjoying the benefits of a contribution made, albeit unwittingly, in the vital early stage of the project. When the Roads Department declared that it could not build an access road quickly or cheaply enough, the Irrigation Department did so – simply by following the elephant trails.

When the Tonga were told in 1955 that they would have to move as the river was about to rise up over their ancestral lands, they scoffed at the notion. They did not believe that Nyaminyami would allow himself to be submerged in deep water, and knowing through generations of experience the ultimate limits that Nyaminyami placed on the fluctuations of the river, they said that it could never happen. And there were occasions during the building of the wall when even the engineers thought they were right. Time after time the river produced the unexpected. But eventually the

setbacks were overcome, the wall was completed and the water began spreading ever wider and deeper over Tonga land. The white men did not gloat over having defeated Nyaminyami. It was said rather that he had changed his mind and had chosen to be submerged.

There is a black stone carving mounted on a plinth overlooking the dam wall from a hill on the southern bank which represents Nyaminyami as a coiled snake with the head of a barbel fish. But for the Tonga, Ka-riwa is still a great black rock lying 130 metres under water, where the Umniati formerly joined the Zambezi.

Now some Tonga say there are two Nyaminyamis – one for the deep water and one for the shallows.

When the waters are blue and unruffled, so that one can gaze deep into the translucence of the lake, they say that Nyaminyami is contented in his situation. But when the sky is black with clouds, and the lake is lustreless and opaque, and dull green waves pound the shoreline into red beaches, they say that he regrets having agreed when he did to live out of reach of the sunlight. And when subterranean readjustments to the unaccustomed weight of water in the basin cause the ground to tremble beneath their feet, they exchange knowing glances.

Twenty years after the dam began to fill, the township built for construction workers on a hilltop 366 metres above the level of the lake is the nucleus of what the guidebooks call the 'Rhodesian Riviera'. The sluiceways in the dam wall still discharge the full flow of the Zambezi down a hundred metres into the gorge below, but where the mnondo-covered slopes meet the lake waters, the old valleys now form coves and inlets which make cosy private harbours for hotels along the shoreline. Speedboats tow waterskiers and transport parties of tourists and anglers to see sights and fight tigerfish, and a two-masted keel yacht bears westward to where the water meets the sky. At night, holidaymakers crowd the gaming tables at the casino, and the dark waters below are dotted with the lights of small boats, where Tonga tribesmen now earn a living in the fishing industry.

Over breakfast on the terrace, one looks out across the border at impassive Zambian hills. The sound of children's laughter drifts up from the swimming pool, and everything seems less menacing here than in the midlands, even if the tourist office does close early for the manager to attend a section leaders' meeting of the police reserve. There haven't been any incidents, he says, since a training camp was established nearby for the Selous Scouts. 'You don't see them during the day, but at night you sometimes see their shadows.'

West of Bumi Hills, patrol boats police a night curfew on the lake. Westward along the lake shore from Kariba, the gneiss escarpment recedes into the Matusadona Mountains, the vegetation on the flats changes, and the skeletal uppermost branches of drowned mopane forests reach up from the water.

'Without these dead trees, Kariba wouldn't be Kariba,' says Jeff Stutchbury. He is speaking of the drowned mopane and the uninhabited reaches of the lake, not of the township.

'People come here and want to blow them all up,' he says. 'They can't see how much a part they are of the whole scene – the brown grass trailing from the branches it was left in when the water was higher, the clouds, the mountains and the complete reflection of it all in the water.'

It is an uncharacteristic day. The lake is pea-soup green and the wind puts white caps on the waves. Low cloud hides the Matusadona Mountain, and in the weak light, the mopane on the flats is the same dull colour as the water.

In a cove below the Bumi Hills, his waterproof jacket zipped and buttoned against the rain, Jeff relaxes in a chair on the broad deck of the catamaran he built for ghosting up to observe lake-edge life. The Tonga named the boat Nakapakapa, because the flapping of its reedmat canopy was like the hovering flight of a pied kingfisher, and Jeff, with a fine sense of what is natural and appropriate, adopted the name.

Jeff Stutchbury wasn't born in Africa, but he never wants to go back to Europe. As a schoolboy in Southampton 40 years ago he dreamed over old maps and leather-bound 'travels' of someday following in the tracks of the African explorers. The War took him out of school to East Africa as a paratrooper. He returned to England only to be demobbed, and twice after that to gaze with distaste at Western man's devastation of his habitat.

He rigged a sail on an old dugout canoe and set out to hunt crocodiles on the islands in Lake Malawi and test his own ability to survive. He back-packed to the Mountains of the Moon, just to look at them, and spent five years eradicating tsetse fly on a remote escarpment in old Northern Rhodesia to save a tribe's cattle from mass slaughter. He fought the fly again in the Zambezi Valley and, when the dam was built, he was one of the Game Department rangers who put five years of their lives into what became known around the world as 'Operation Noah'; saving 6 000 animals stranded on hilltop islands in the rising waters.

'Sometimes the trees were dripping with snakes and there were sheets of ants on the water,' he recalls.

Jeff has been 30 years in Africa, 20 of them associated with Lake Kariba. As ranger, crocodile farmer and Safari leader, he has lived on its shores, on its islands and on its waters, probing the mouths of its tributaries, exploring in wonder the evolving life of the lake.

'For 18 years these old mopanes have been in the water,' he says. 'This is a big body of water. They take a heavy pounding. They have shed their bark, and the thinner branches have snapped off and floated away, but the heartwood remains as tough as ever. I have seen trees like these that have been more than 30 years in dams. I am out among them almost every day and I see very little depletion. They take on a new life in the water. They're a haven for birdlife, and the fishermen who want to blow them up don't realise that the fish are where the trees are.'

Jeff speaks with the same understanding about the Kariba weed that is cursed by speedboat men for fouling their propellors and barring their passage. 'Without the weed, there'd be no panicum grass,' he says, 'and without panicum there'd be far less wildlife.

'They said the weed was getting out of hand and brought a grasshopper from South America to try to keep it down. But there wasn't too much of it. The lake had only just begun. Now that it is full, the waves pound the weed, break it up and sink it, or throw it up far inland, destroying it and, at the same time, creating something new – a panicum grassland.'

The panicum, he explains, is a swamp grass which, like the weed, originates high up in the Zambezi-Chobe river system. Fish nibble away the soft part above the roots, the blades float up, become embroiled with the weed and are carried with it down the Zambezi into the lake, where the wind gathers the weed into floating 'islands' along the shoreline. When the lake rises after the rains, the water carries weed and panicum inland and leaves them stranded when it recedes in the dry season. There the panicum is mulched into the dead weed and takes root. Thereafter, the rise and fall of the lake give it the annual dunking it needs. Where the rising water-table meets the streams flowing from the escarpment, silt is deposited which facilitates further establishment of the grass, which in turn stabilises the soil.

Here along the shoreline of Lake Kariba one can witness and take part in what no other place has to offer: the evolution of an entirely new African wildlife ecology.

Before the lake was created, many of the animals in this area used to move annually in the dry season down into the Zambezi Valley. Now they remain in the vicinity all year round, feeding on the panicum when the lake level is low and the bush is dry, and moving back into the bush after the rains, when the lake rises over the grassland.

The animals are constantly adapting to the changes in order to survive. Buffalo, impala and hippo thrive on the panicum. Elephant take advantage of the green bite at a time of year when they would normally have browsed, and so more trees have an opportunity to grow. Stabilised conditions have favoured better breeding. There is now a localised rainfall that there never was before for 16 kilometres inland of the escarpment. Beaches have formed so that crocodiles, who fared very badly at first, now have sandbanks on which to lay their eggs. The fish eagle population has increased, seagulls and terns show up in increasing number. Many birds not seen in the area before, such as the woodland kingfisher, have made their nests in the virile vegetation along the waterways. Stutchbury has identified over 130 species, and on his stealthy visits to the Bumi River, he is continually adding to his list – cormorants, storks, geese, ducks, vultures, cranes, parrots, kingfishers, bee-eaters, hornbills, oxpeckers, firefinches, woodpeckers and hoopoes, the snake eagle, the hawk eagle and the martial eagle . . .

'The lake has established itself very quickly – although the shoreline was the result of an act of man, it has the aura of being completely natural.'

'It's all there,' says Jeff. 'Nature is taking over what man has created and is moulding it to her way.' He is where he wants to be.

Malindidzimu comes to Great Zimbabwe

Chisingaperi chine manenji
A thing without end is mysterious *Shona proverb*

A few kilometres outside the modern city of Bulawayo the ruins of the old Ndebele capital of the same name have long since disappeared beneath billiard-table lawns, jacaranda-lined avenues, tennis courts, rose gardens and asphalted pathways bordered by low hedges and shin-high white picket fences. The warm autumn air bears the sound of powered mowers, the snip of garden shears and rhythmic tick of revolving water jets.

Here 20 000 Ndebele once lived at Lobengula's royal kraal within sight of the great flat-topped hill called Thaba Induna. It is from this hill that Mzilikazi, Lobengula's father, is reputed to have hurled to their deaths 12 indunas whom he believed had plotted against him. Where Lobengula once kraaled his goats stand the white walls of Government House. Here, too, the small thatched rondavel which Rhodes had his men build for him on the spot where Lobengula slept has been preserved. The only relic of the former capital is the Indaba Tree in whose shade the Ndebele king held court and signed the fateful Moffat Treaty that became the first stepping stone to the white man's conquest of the Rhodesian plateau. Today the tree is dying of old age, but from its roots have sprung new young roots that will eventually replace it.

At the entrance to the grounds of Government House a sculptured British South Africa Company lion stands triumphant on a fallen Ndebele shield. But now hornets build their nests in the bronze curls of the lion's mane. Much water has flowed through Bulawayo Spruit since the Company flag was first raised above a tree on its bank.

The territory was ruled under Company administration by a legislative council, but in 1923 petitions by the 29 white settlers resulted in it being annexed to Britain, who granted the settlers Responsible Government. The new government bought out the Company's mineral rights to Rhodesia for two million pounds and the easy flow of settler life, interrupted only by involvement on distant battlefields in the Second World War, continued until after the war. Then, in 1949, the leaders of what were at that time Northern Rhodesia, Southern Rhodesia and Nyasaland met at Victoria Falls to discuss a federation of the three territories which they felt could be to their mutual advantage.

The Federation of Rhodesia and Nyasaland became a reality in 1954, but before the end of the next decade, mounting black militancy against apparent inequalities began to herald the dissolution of Federation. It broke up officially on the last day of 1963. Northern Rhodesia and Nyasaland received their independence and became Zambia and Malawi, but the negotiation of Southern Rhodesian independence was deadlocked on the question of black political advancement. Southern Rhodesia had the largest number of whites and their financial stake in the country was such that they refused to contemplate relinquishing power, even gradually, to the black majority and were not prepared to accept a constitution that would pave the way for majority rule. And so independence was withheld by Britain.

Settler discontent culminated in 1965 when Southern Rhodesia unilaterally declared itself independent. Black, British and international reaction was swift and sharp. Britain imposed a total trade embargo and the United Nations imposed oil sanctions. Within the country, rising expectations, stimulated by developments in neighbouring territories but frustrated at home, carried black resistance into a new phase: the following year the first isolated shots were fired in the bush war that over the next 12 years would spread to every part of the country.

Under the pressures of escalating war and economic isolation, the whites are reaching a point where their only course for survival is the acceptance of far more than they had been asked to concede in 1963. Majority rule based on 'one man one vote' elections is now inevitable.

Bulawayo is built in a position which in former times commanded the only practical approach to the central Rhodesian plateau from the south. In this position it has often been a battleground. The modern city retains something of a military flavour. The wide streets that were intended to be broad enough for a wagon drawn by a team of 24 oxen to turn suggest that early town planners were also influenced by visions of Imperial Rome. Long low buildings of red brick and stone with ornate façades in the barrack baroque style of the outposts of empire intersperse modern office blocks and modest skyscrapers. But the imperial charms of Bulawayo have faded over the years. There is an easy-going air about the city, as if it is relieved that it no longer needs to maintain pretensions. There is a Royal Hotel, but the only other reference to empire is the signboard outside a hairdressing salon.

The present war seems to have touched Bulawayo least of all the Rhodesian cities. The old well, sunk to provide the citizens with water when they went into laager for several months during the 1896 Ndebele rebellion, now supplies a fountain in front of the City Hall. A memorial plaque reads: 'To the honour and glory of the 1893 columns. These pioneers still live within the land they won.'

In the Matopo Hills, south of the city, the spirit of Rhodesia's founder still resides on the hill called Malindidzimu, among the spirits who guard the grave of Mzilikazi on Ntumbane Hill. The Shona say that when one settles in a new place one must learn to know the older spirits of the land and accord them due respect because they are often the most potent.

Today the heirs of the spirits of Malindidzimu, Ntumbane and Great Zimbabwe are competing for the Rhodesian legacy.

Dzimba dzinotsva dzakavimbikana
Huts that are close burn down at the same time
Shona proverb

Kuturika denga remba/kubatirana
To put a roof onto the walls of a hut, hands must join
Shona proverb

THE PHOTOGRAPHS
MATOPOS
ZIMBABWE
KARIBA
AFRICAN VILLAGE
EASTERN HIGHLANDS
WANKIE
CHIMANIMANI
VICTORIA FALLS
TRANSITION

The natural granite domes and castles of the Matopo Hills, which rise abruptly from the mopane lowveld south of Bulawayo, are hallowed in the history and spiritual life of most Rhodesians. So sacred are some of the hills that they may not be pointed at, while the names of many are in ancient dialects and have been so

MATOPOS

distorted by speakers of other languages that their meaning has been lost. Here early Bushmen celebrated nature by painting their cave walls, and here followers of the Shona cult of the Great God, Mwari, still have their most sacred 'rain cave', to which both Ndebele chiefs and white farmers send tribute.

The Matopos are the burial place of Mzilikazi, founder of the Ndebele nation, and Cecil John Rhodes, who founded Rhodesia – Mzilikazi in a cave on Ntumbane Hill, Rhodes in a crypt hewn in the dome of Malindidzimu, dwelling place of the spirits that guard Mzilikazi's grave.

Mzilikazi gave the hills their name, calling them *Matobo,* the bald ones, because they looked to him like an assembly of bald-headed indunas.

Rhodes first thought of burial here after visiting Mzilikazi's cave to investigate Ndebele complaints that his troopers had desecrated the king's grave.

When, in the 1896 rebellion, the Ndebele could no longer resist British supremacy in open country, they withdrew into the Matopos, believing they could hold out there indefinitely. To end the stalemate, Rhodes went unarmed into the area and, in a series of indabas, convinced the Ndebele indunas that they could not win. They laid down their arms and, without a king since the death of Lobengula three years before, they gave Rhodes the praise-name *Lamula Mkunzi* – 'he who separated the fighting bulls'.

He acquired an estate in the Matopos and lived near the Ndebele for a time. Out riding one morning, he came upon the hill Malindidzimu. He called it 'View of the World', and unaware of the rôle of its spirits, he chose it for his grave.

Thirty-four years after Mzilikazi's death, Rhodes died in Cape Town on March 26, 1902. He ended his last journey on April 10 in a teak coffin, hauled by 12 black oxen on a gun carriage up Malindidzimu. Respecting Ndebele fears that shots might disturb the spirits, none were fired, and the assembled chiefs spontaneously substituted the royal salute, '*Bayete!*', addressing it for the first time to a white man. And so, Rhodes joined the spirit guardians of Mzilikazi on Malindidzimu, and from that time the custodians at his grave have been Ndebele.

White Rhodesians still feel about Rhodes as Rudyard Kipling did:

> Living he was the land, and dead
> His soul shall be her soul.

In 1953, on the centenary of his birth, over a million hectares were declared the Rhodes Matopos National Park, and today giraffe, zebra, buffalo and wildebeest, impala, eland, sable and white rhinoceros roam here as they did when this was still the Bushman's domain.

1 . . . I desire to be buried in the Matopos on the hill which I used to visit and which I called a 'View of the World', in a square to be cut in the top of the hill, covered with a plain brass plate with the words thereon: 'Here lie the remains of Cecil John Rhodes.'
2 The 'castle kopjes' of the Matopos loom like fortresses built by giant hands.
3 British-born widower, Mr C. G. Fryer, who keeps a small trading store in the southern Matopos, where virtually his only human contact is with his African customers, displays the medals and citations he earned fighting for Britain in both World Wars.
4, 5 The magnificent domes and spires of the Matopos are the result of splitting and erosion along lines of weakness inherent in the granite. These weaknesses have produced two characteristic forms: the whaleback 'dwalas' (4) evolved by 'onion-skin' weathering of the rock surface, and the heaped boulders of the 'castle kopjes'.

6 *'The chaotic grandeur of it all!' exclaimed Rhodes when he first saw these hills.*

7 *Part of the weathering process, the probing roots of a tree split the mother-rock.*

8 *The snap of a twig, a rustling of cloth, the faintest scent of possible danger . . . an impala ewe senses an intruder.*

9 *The hulking white rhinoceros, largest living land mammal after the elephant, is represented in Bushman rock art in the Matopos, but was for many years extinct in Rhodesia. Reintroduced from wildlife reserves elsewhere, they are again breeding in the Rhodes Matopos National Park.*

10 *The presence of 'a wandering spirit' which Rhodes sensed in the Matopos, is strongest when the landscape assumes its dry-season tints, where broken brown hillsides flank yellow grassy valleys and great granite dwalas on the skyline lead on to new horizons.*

9

They call it Lake Kariba, although it is really a dam – one of the largest in the world: 282 kilometres long, 42 kilometres wide at its broadest, and covering 5 180 square kilometres of what was formerly the Gwembe trough and the bed of the Zambezi. Kariba nevertheless has the appearance of a true Central African lake,

KARIBA

but with a character uniquely its own. It was created in the mid-fifties with the single purpose of giving hydro-electric power to Rhodesia and Zambia, at a time when the two countries were still the southern and northern components of the Federation of Rhodesia and Nyasaland. Because it is man-made some conservationists have been slow to show interest in the lake, but it is artificial only in the sense that it came into being when man built a wall across the narrow entrance to Kariba Gorge and held back the river. Indeed, the environment of the lake has been fashioned by nature itself, adapting to the initial inundation and then to the annual fluctuations of the lake level, developing into a rich habitat for a diversity of wildlife along its shoreline and within its waters.

Part of this evolving habitat has been the water fern, *Salvinia auriculata,* brought by the Zambezi from its upper drainage area. It collected and underwent explosive growth in the lake which caused alarm when, in 1962, it was found to cover more than 20 percent of the surface, but natural agents have since greatly contained it, confining the *Salvinia* to creeks and inlets, and ecologists now recognise its rôle in stabilising the lake shore.

During the early years of the lake, the *Salvinia* held the nutrients released by the newly-flooded land and, in the absence of rooted aquatic vegetation, provided food organisms and cover for young fish. Wind and wave concentrate it at the lake edge when the water is high, and it is left behind when the water level drops some nine metres by the end of the dry season. The *Salvinia* brings with it from the Upper Zambezi the stalks of a swamp grass, *Panicum repens,* which takes root in the *Salvinia* stranded by the retreating water and establishes a grassland, which is the basis of a new ecosystem in this new environment.

All through the night lights play on the water as commercial fishermen in small boats set their nets for the shoals of sardine-like kapenta. It is estimated that as much as 10 000 tons could be taken annually from the lake without overfishing. The catch, either frozen or sun-dried, is a popular and rich source of protein among black Rhodesians.

For conservationists, 'Operation Noah', the dramatic rescue of some 6 000 animals of 35 species from disappearing hilltop islands while the lake was filling, afforded a rare opportunity for gathering scientific information about Central African mammals.

Today, it is the evolving ecology of the shoreline that fascinates and demonstrates that man, at the same time as serving his own needs, can himself be a constructive force of nature.

12

13

11 *Touched by the late afternoon sun, the exposed upper branches of a submerged mopane forest are a distinctive feature of the lake edge. These drowned trees provided a substitute for rooted aquatic vegetation before it appeared, and an alternative habitat for underwater life once it had.*
12-15 *A multitude of birds have been attracted to the new shoreline: over 130 species have been observed in the Matusadona Flats area alone. Here saddlebills lift ponderously from drowned mopane at the water's edge (12); a weaver tends its nest (13); a woodland kingfisher adds its loud trilled call to the sounds of the lake (14); and a solitary goliath heron surveys its waterside domain.*

16, 17 *Game-viewers observed. Not a muscle stirs as an impala ram (16) watches from a thicket.*
18 *A sudden flash of white against tree and sky as an egret comes to roost.*
19 *White-breasted cormorants on 'phantom' mopane hung with dried grass by the seasonally receding waters. Individual birds return continually to the same perch and their droppings streak the dead branches.*

20 *Tough customers in a tight spot, Cape buffalo have no enemies apart from lion and man. Although some old bulls live alone, the buffalo usually range in large herds, drinking and grazing by night and hiding themselves in thick vegetation by day.*

21 *A fish eagle on the hunt spreads its wings. The compelling call of these birds haunts Africa's wetlands.*

22 *When the lake was filling and there were no sandbanks the hippo were displaced, but they preside once more over the backwaters. Most of their day is spent in the water where they often submerge for up to six minutes, walking freely about on the bottom as their specific gravity is higher than that of water. At night they emerge to forage far from their daytime refuge.*

23 Only the upper branches of these dead trees will be visible above the lake surface when it is full, but when the level falls during the dry season Panicum grass takes over the exposed shoreline and lures elephant from the bush to graze at the water's edge.

24 A young tusker emerges from a dip in the lake.

25, 26 Elephant still follow the paths that were used before the water rose, but where once they walked they must now swim to feed on islands that were formerly the tops of kopjes.

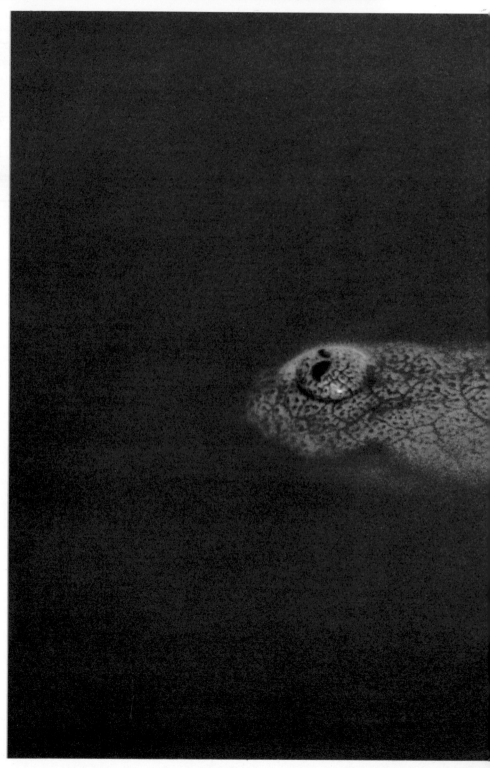

27 *A crocodile lunging on the attack evokes fears that echo the primordial struggle for supremacy between reptiles and mammals.*
28 *Claw on claw, crocodiles bask in the sun.*
29 *Neither cruel nor malevolent, the gleam in the crocodile's eye is no more than a cold appraisal of its next meal.*

30, 31 *Slow boats, powered by almost silent engines, afford the best means of combining gameviewing with fishing along the shoreline. The fish which may be caught in the lake include the fighting tiger-fish, Hunyani salmon, four varieties of bream, chessa, inkupi, bottlenose and barbel.*

32 *With only two floodgates open, 180 million litres a minute thunder into Kariba Gorge below the dam wall. All six would release 540 million litres – some 200 million more than the peak flow over the Victoria Falls.*

The arched wall, retaining 185 000 million cubic metres of lake water, measures 633 metres from bank to bank along its crest and is 131 metres high in midstream. Over a million cubic metres of concrete and nearly 11 000 tons of reinforcing steel went into its construction.

The economic importance of the lake to Rhodesia is its potential for delivering 8 500 million kilowatt hours of electrical power a year, its annual yields of more than 4 000 tons of fish, and the tourist industry that has developed at its eastern end.

European fantasy has attributed the Zimbabwe Ruins capriciously to the ancient Phoenicians, the Persians, the Arabs and even the Portuguese on no more than speculative grounds. All the stone structures at Great Zimbabwe, however, were erected between the latter part of the twelfth and the close of the fourteenth

ZIMBABWE

centuries – long after the Phoenicians had ceased to exist, and before the Portuguese arrived on the East African coast. While Arab traders probably visited Great Zimbabwe while building was in progress, there is no evidence to suggest that they were ever there in large numbers, remained there continuously for any length of time or influenced the style and techniques of building. But the masonry does disclose a chain of locally evolved technical innovation through two centuries, which links the most primitive stone structures with the most sophisticated, and archaeologists are today generally agreed that the builders were indigenous people – ancestors of the present-day Shona.

Great Zimbabwe, with 12 separate groups of buildings spread over 40 hectares, is by far the largest of some 200 stone building complexes belonging to the same tradition that are scattered over the Rhodesian plateau.

Although the stone walls resemble fortifications, the builders' disregard for natural defensive features indicates that they were not erected for defensive purposes. A combination of established facts, circumstantial evidence and informed guess-work proposes that they were constructed as prestige dwellings for a ruling élite, who had grown wealthy from acting as middlemen in the two-way trade between the gold-producing areas of the interior and the coast.

At Great Zimbabwe, the first walls of the Hill Ruin, fatuously named The Acropolis, do not give the impression that the masons had imported any knowledge of their craft from established stone-building traditions elsewhere. The coursing is irregular and only the outer skins of the walls are constructed of roughly squared blocks, while the insides are filled with irregularly shaped pieces of rock.

By the end of the thirteenth century, the number of individuals who could afford prestige dwellings had increased, and building, in the same style as on the hill, commenced in the valley below. The economic prosperity of Great Zimbabwe reached its peak in the fourteenth century, when it became the centre of an extensive trading empire. New crafts, such as goldsmithing, stone carving and the spinning and weaving of cotton, were developed.

The Valley Ruins built in this period show a steady refinement of the skill of the masons, which culminated in the construction of the outer wall of the great Elliptical Enclosure and its Conical Tower. The ground was levelled to provide an even foundation, drainage was built in and the granite building blocks were sorted into like sizes to facilitate regular coursing, inside as well as on the outer surfaces of the wall, which was tapered towards the top, and to which purely decorative features were added.

33 *Early European visitors to the Ruins thought that the Conical Tower at the focus of the Elliptical Enclosure must have had some association with phallic worship. Both the shape and tradition suggest, however, that it was intended to represent a Shona grain bin, symbolising the sovereign right of the ruling Mambo to receive produce of the land as tribute from his subjects.*

34, 35, 36 *The massive outer wall of the Elliptical Enclosure and the Conical Tower it contains are products of the final building phase at Great Zimbabwe. Erected in the middle of the fourteenth century, the regular coursing (35) reflects the evolved skill of local masons, which found its ultimate expression in the chevron pattern (36) built into the upper courses on the outside of the wall behind the Conical Tower.*

37 *A later extension to an earlier wall inside the Elliptical Enclosure displays four double courses of black stone (left) decoratively interspersed with the upper granite courses.*

38 *The walled passage on the ascent to the Hill Ruin shows the less developed masonry techniques used in earlier structures. The monoliths projecting from the top of the wall of the Western Enclosure on the hill are believed to have represented the ancestors of the ruling lineage, who were venerated as guardian tribal spirits by the whole people.*

39-43 *Erected in the twelfth century, the earliest stone structures on the hill appear to have been intended as extensions to the natural shelter afforded by the existing granite boulders. Continuous wall-building created a number of distinct ritual, residential and functional areas, connected by passages and stairways.*

37 38

40

41

42

43

A small cluster of grass-roofed huts somewhere in the countryside has been both home and community to the vast majority of people in Rhodesia at some stage in their lives, but today the tiny scattered villages are a fading feature of the changing rural scene. In many areas, although the huts are still standing, the children who

AFRICAN VILLAGE

once played in the sand outside them have vanished.

Ancestor spirits of former inhabitants may linger yet among the ruins, but the people have moved away. It would be wrong however to assume that these villages and homesteads represent a way of life that had remained unchanged throughout the centuries. As long as man has dwelt in this land between the Limpopo and Zambezi rivers, his social system and way of life have been evolving and changing, albeit slowly and fitfully. But since Europeans began settling here in the 1890s and introduced innovations such as a cash economy and urban culture, the old order has been placed under ever-increasing pressure for change. More recently, the population explosion and the bush war have further forced the pace.

The small traditional village, consisting of the headman, his family and other families linked to him by ties of kinship or other common bonds, was a place where the warmth of domestic life extended into community life, and the headman was looked upon as the father of all who lived under him. Outsiders who joined the little society were as much part of it as the headman's own family. They became permanent members from the moment they were allocated land to cultivate and could not afterwards be ejected.

In the old days, among the Shona, all land belonged to the chief whose right to it was believed to have been granted by the great god, Mwari. The chief distributed it among his people and collected tribute from it. What is more, as sole living link with his chiefly ancestors, he was a ritual leader who could intervene on behalf of his followers and kinsmen with the guardians of the spirit world.

Under European rule, however, ultimate sovereignty over the land was shifted to the Government, and thus one of the essential elements of chiefly authority was removed. Christianity offered an alternative to the ancestor cult and this source of authority among the chiefs was also weakened. The large number of migrant workers away from home at any one time has led to divided loyalties between traditional and political leaders. Declared townships, business centres and large enterprises in tribal areas are outside the chiefs' jurisdiction and so the chiefly rôle has consistently lost ground to the new social forces at play.

The bush war has meant that black people in many tribal areas have been brought from their scattered homesteads to live in protected villages, partly to shelter those who do not want to co-operate with the insurgents and partly to restrict those who do. And while many of these people look forward to the day when they will be able to resume their traditional form of village life, it is more likely that when the time comes an entirely new pattern of life will take its place.

44 *Granite boulders dominating a cluster of Karanga huts seem to preserve the proper scale of man and nature.*

45 *In the early morning outside a rural homestead little girls play in the cooking area. From the age of four they are encouraged to make a game of their traditional chores about the cooking fire – helping to collect firewood, pounding maize into meal for porridge, caring for the chickens that forever scuffle and scratch for food in the neatly swept yards, and preparing the family meals. In the rural areas 'mealie meal' porridge known as sadza is the staple food eaten with a variety of vegetable 'relishes' and, on special occasions, meat. Goats and chickens are sometimes slaughtered and with luck small game may help fill the pot, but cattle are killed and eaten only on ritually important occasions.*

46 *The grace with which black women carry heavy loads on their heads often gives the impression that there is no effort involved, but beads of perspiration tell the true story.*

47 *The need for firewood has stripped this village area of shrubs and trees. Here, after a shower of rain, a dog takes shelter under the eaves of a hut.*

48 *When the heavens open, even the ducks may look forlorn, but a houseproud woman seizes the opportunity to put a sparkle into her kitchenware. In the past all her utensils would have been made in the village from clay or wood, but today she prefers the goods offered at the trading store.*

49 *In the cool interior of a hut villagers enjoy easy companionship. Even here urban influences are visible in the style of dress and an increasing array of factory-made items.*

50 *Many an urban dweller once herded his father's cattle. Traditionally a man's herds are his single greatest symbol of wealth and status, and cattle continue to play this important rôle in many of Rhodesia's rural areas.*

52

51 *Outside the towns 'leg power' remains the commonest form of transport. Here women, babies slung on their backs, ford the Sabi River.*

52, 53, 56 *Firewood and water must often be collected far from the villages and it is the work of the women to do so. They carry the immense loads of wood and bulky water containers on their heads.*

54, 55 *Standing passengers lurch helplessly, chickens squawk underfoot and the passing countryside vanishes behind one in a cloud of yellow dust, but as a test of endurance, nothing can compare with a country bus-ride. The final destination is often little more than a hand-lettered sign on a tree (55).*

44 *Granite boulders dominating a cluster of Karanga huts seem to preserve the proper scale of man and nature.*

45 *In the early morning outside a rural homestead little girls play in the cooking area. From the age of four they are encouraged to make a game of their traditional chores about the cooking fire – helping to collect firewood, pounding maize into meal for porridge, caring for the chickens that forever scuffle and scratch for food in the neatly swept yards, and preparing the family meals. In the rural areas 'mealie meal' porridge known as sadza is the staple food eaten with a variety of vegetable 'relishes' and, on special occasions, meat. Goats and chickens are sometimes slaughtered and with luck small game may help fill the pot, but cattle are killed and eaten only on ritually important occasions.*

46 *The grace with which black women carry heavy loads on their heads often gives the impression that there is no effort involved, but beads of perspiration tell the true story.*

47 *The need for firewood has stripped this village area of shrubs and trees. Here, after a shower of rain, a dog takes shelter under the eaves of a hut.*

48 *When the heavens open, even the ducks may look forlorn, but a houseproud woman seizes the opportunity to put a sparkle into her kitchenware. In the past all her utensils would have been made in the village from clay or wood, but today she prefers the goods offered at the trading store.*

49 *In the cool interior of a hut villagers enjoy easy companionship. Even here urban influences are visible in the style of dress and an increasing array of factory-made items.*

50 *Many an urban dweller once herded his father's cattle. Traditionally a man's herds are his single greatest symbol of wealth and status, and cattle continue to play this important rôle in many of Rhodesia's rural areas.*

57 *The freedom of the fields that was taken for granted seems suddenly appealing when it must be forsaken to prepare for a place in a changing world.*

58, 59 *Even in remote villages there is often a school offering a basic education.*

60 *When she grows up this little village girl will probably seek a future in the towns.*

61 *'This is the end' proclaims graffiti scrawled on a village door.*

59

60

61

62 – 66 *All else is forgotten when the drumbeats sound. Hands clap, whistles blow, bodies start to sway, and soon feet are pounding out the rhythm, whether in an appeal for rain, in celebration of a good harvest or simply for the pleasure of dancing.*

62 65

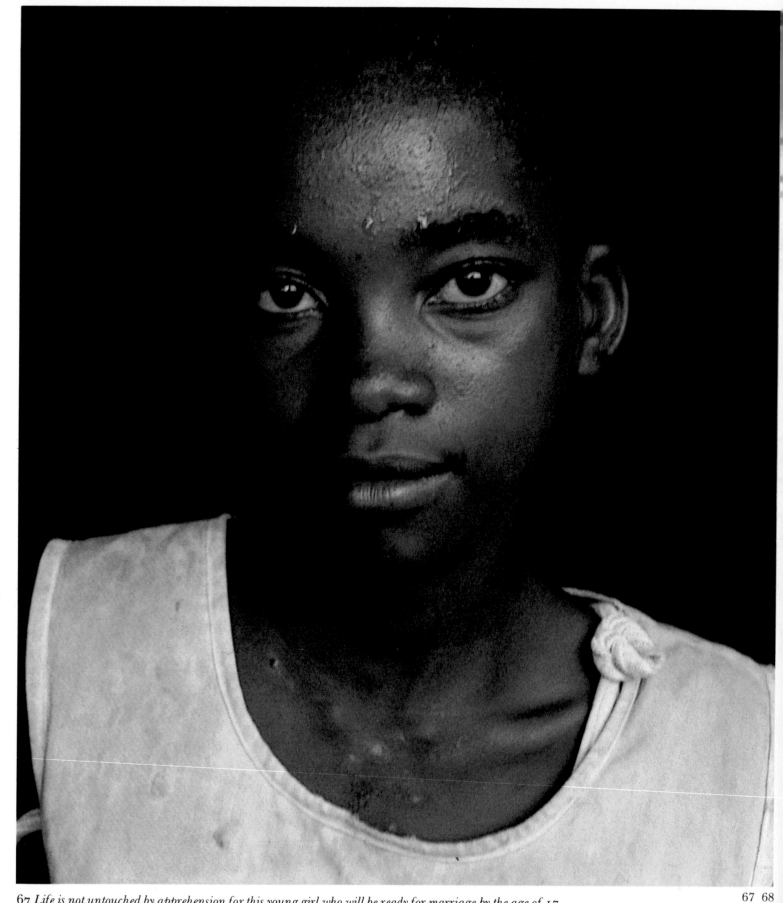

67 *Life is not untouched by apprehension for this young girl who will be ready for marriage by the age of 17. Traditionally the choice of spouse will not depend on her but on her family.*
68 *A young man who has spent some time in the city is a hero to young boys who have never been beyond the village fields.*
69 *On the Sabi River, a boat affords this man an opportunity to be alone with himself while at the same time providing food for his family.*

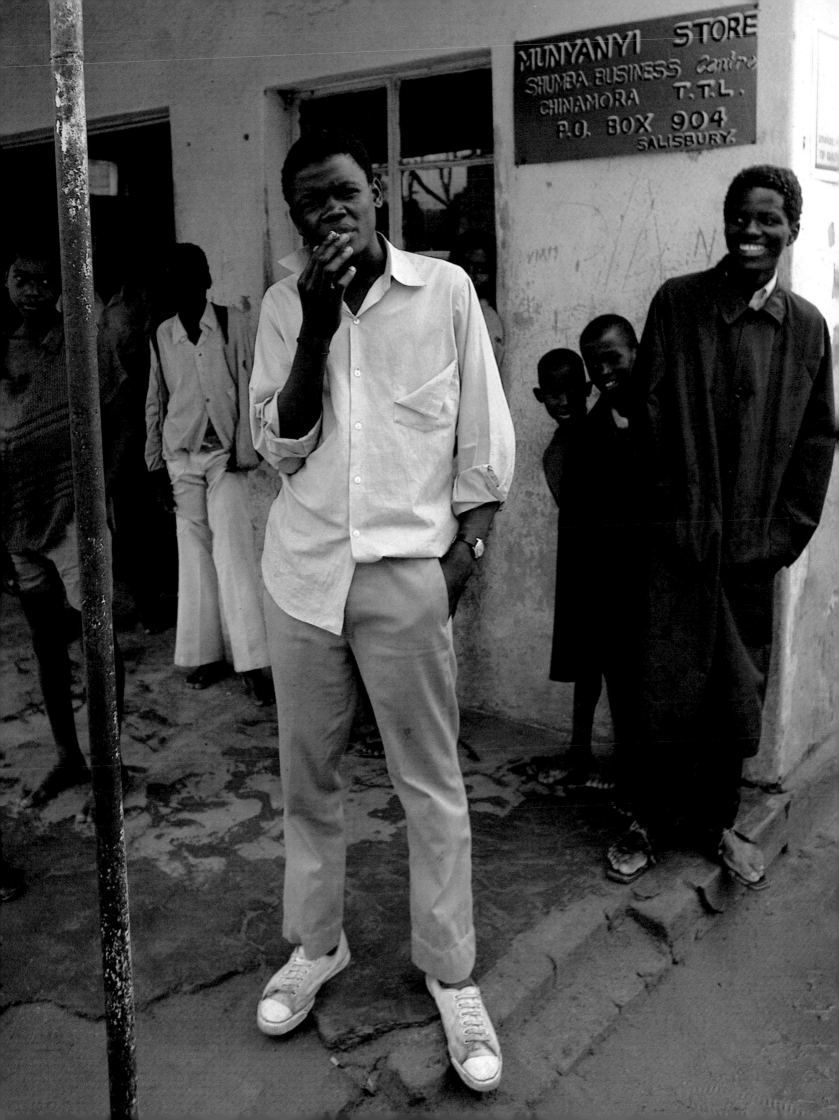

70 *An old Tonga in the Zambezi Valley. The chicken-run in the*
background is built on stilts to help keep out predators.
71 *A baboon skull hanging outside a Tonga granary hut is a warning to*
would-be marauders of what befell another of their kind.
72 *The inevitable chickens find shade outside a hut.*
73 *Spirits, witches, sorcerers and diviners are an integral part of the*
Shona world. This n'anga or diviner went into a deep trance as she
sought to help a patient. While in this state she spoke in a deep voice
words unintelligible to those who came to be treated. Traditional healers
and diviners deal with both physical and psychic problems and have a
remarkable knowledge of the medicinal properties of trees and plants.

72

On the highest mountain in Rhodesia, there once lived a famous medicine-man, a *n'anga,* so widely renowned for his treatment of physical and psychic disorders that the district came to be known as Inyanga, and the loftiest peak was named Inyangani. The old wonder-worker has long been dead, but Inyanga has lost none

EASTERN HIGHLANDS

of its magic. Here cool temperatures and perennial mists and showers, brought by winds from the Indian Ocean, have created an enchanted land of herb-scented alpine breezes, thick forests and rolling downs, effervescent streams and crystal waterfalls.

Inyangani, rising 2 594 metres above sea-level, is towards the northern end of a chain of high mountains which forms the country's eastern ramparts. But for a narrow causeway along the watershed, these highlands of the Manicaland province have, over many millions of years, been separated from the central plateau by heavy erosion into the Sabi and Zambezi. They have developed in partial isolation from the rest of the country, with a distinctive climate, vegetation pattern, history and agriculture.

Formerly a Bushman stronghold, Inyanga became for several centuries the home of one of the earliest Iron Age peoples in Rhodesia. Later, refugees from Zimba raiders and Portuguese freebooters left the ruins of stone forts, sunken goat kraals and terraced hillsides scattered over 5 000 square kilometres in this area.

The thick dolerite upper-shelf of Inyangani gives way to granite foothills where the range is cut to the south of it by the Honde River. Here the closed forests of the uplands are interrupted by a belt of msasa- and mnondo-dominated woodland.

There is a second break in the range at Umtali, where the valley gives natural access from the lowlands of Mozambique to the Rhodesian interior. This was the route taken by the first Portuguese adventurers who came up from the coast in search of the source of Manyika gold, and it was here that much later the British built their rail outlet to the sea.

South-east of present-day Umtali, the lingering mists gave their name to the Vumba and here in the seventeenth century the Portuguese established a permanent trade fair.

Although the gold deposits in the Eastern Highlands have never been as rewarding as those in the interior, they have been worked successively by tribesman, Portuguese fortune hunter, British colonist and Rhodesian.

But if it was gold that first attracted strangers to the Eastern Highlands, it is not what kept them there. Today, the tea and coffee estates that run down to the border, the pine, wattle and gum plantations that cover vast expanses of hillside, and the orchards and market gardens that thrive in the fertile valleys, extract far richer returns from the soil than the stamping mill at the Rezende Mine.

That they remain here, in what has become a volatile war zone, is proof that the spell of the mountains is still powerful magic.

74 *The Vumba overlooks a rugged mountainland in which bare rocky peaks and msasa-covered slopes seclude small cultivated valleys.*
75 *A shower passes, the clouds open and a village on a verdant hill is spotlighted by the sun against the dark backdrop of the mountain.*
76 *Aging timbers of the long-silent stamping mill at the Rezende Mine recall gold-pioneering days at Penhalonga. The Iberian connection with gold in this region is preserved in the names of both the town and the mine which were called after the Portuguese counts who established them. When it became uneconomical in the 1960s work was suspended here for*

several years, but improved gold prices, better technology and Government incentives have once again brought the old mine into operation, continuing a tradition that dates from the first Monomatapa.
77 *Many a prospector must have imagined his future assured when the dull lustre of 'fool's gold' caught his eye. But beneath the chimerical gleam on this old dump a residue of gold remains to be extracted by modern methods.*
78 *Scarred and worn, a granite foothill bulks large over a quiet valley in the Eastern Highlands.*

78

79

80

81

79-82 *Rain in all seasons creates a wonderland of running and falling waters in the Inyanga uplands.*
83 *An early morning mist lingering over a pine plantation in the Eastern Highlands heightens the seeming incongruity of such scenery within the Tropics.*

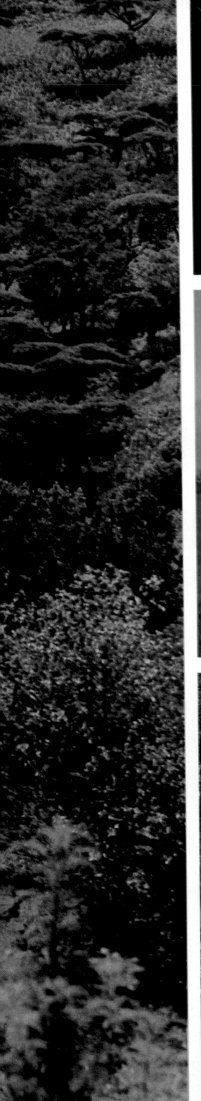

85
86

84 *West of Inyanga the closed forests thin out into wooded grassland and small cultivated fields hug the open spaces.*

85 *It's 'msasa time' in Rhodesia when these trees put out their new red leaves in early spring.*

86 *The kafferboom, which bears the lucky bean, is aflame with scarlet flowers from July to November. According to African medicine and folklore, infusions from the bark and leaf are believed to ease complaints as diverse as the pains of childbirth, sprains and ear-ache, while the crushed leaves are a popular remedy for suppurating sores.*

87 *The naturalised Australian gums north of Penhalonga are reputed to be among the tallest and straightest in the world.*

87

88 *A domestic dispute, or perhaps the arrival of powerful strangers in the land, immortalised by a Bushman artist in one of the many rock art sites in the Eastern Highlands. Rhodesia is widely and richly endowed with the work of Bushmen who have left on rock surfaces throughout the country evidence not only of their way of life but also a fascinating visual record of the development of their art from the simple monochrome silhouettes of early pictures to the vibrant multi-coloured celebration of later works. In the careful detail of some Rhodesian Bushman pictures one can only wonder at the remarkably keen powers of observation on the part of the artists. While experts still argue the motivation for much of the work, 'art for art's sake' must seem a partial explanation to anyone who has marvelled at the vigour and spontaneity of Bushman art at its best.*
89 *A superb natural stronghold, this one-time Bushman refuge commands a view of every approach to the valley.*
90 *A haze tempers the colours of a highland sunset.*

88
89

Once the final Rozwi refuge from Ndebele impis, Wankie was later Mzilikazi's royal hunting preserve. A mecca for the white hunters who blazed the first trails northward, it was also the place where the last Rhodesian Bushmen clung to their ways, until it was proclaimed a game reserve in 1928 and hunting for survival

WANKIE

became punishable as poaching. Unrivalled since 1932 as the country's major national park, its 1,5 million hectares lie across a watershed, draining north into the Zambezi and south-west towards the Makgadikgadi Pan in central Botswana. In a wetter age, when mudflats were spread over the extreme south-west of the present park, and when swamps and forests in the north laid down the Wankie coalfields, great rivers flowed here. The shallow soils north of the watershed today support mopane woodland, baobab in rocky areas, and monkey thorn, sausage tree, knob thorn and splendid acacia beside the Lukozi River, while in the north-west, tree wistarias fringe grassy vleis between basalt outcrops.

Ancient dunes, now thickly vegetated, tell of a remote dry period when Wankie was a sand desert, and two thirds of the park, south and west of the watershed, are still covered with Kalahari sand hundred of metres deep. Here woodlands and vleis mingle with mangwe scrub and open grassland. In the east, at the heads of the once-great rivers, better soils nourish sweet grazing lands and stands of Rhodesian teak and mahogany, flowering mukusi and umTshibi, bloodwood and manketti, which bears the African almond that, roasted in a warthog intestine over coals, is a favourite Bushman dish.

When the rains come, the sandveld is verdant with grass and foliage and water fills every hollow. Here gemsbok, hartebeest, wildebeest and giraffe of the dry savanna rub shoulders with waterbuck, reedbuck, buffalo, elephant and zebra which migrate into these parts during the wet months of summer. In winter, when drought strips the veld of its greenery and the surface water dries up, these animals will disperse once more to their rivers. But the animals of the sandveld remain, surviving on the water in the pans and vleis they themselves have created by centuries of digging in the calcrete areas along the watershed, eating soil for the mineral salts it contains, carrying it off as mud caked on their hides, and simply by drinking the muddy water. By this means alone one elephant may remove five tons of soil a year from a pan.

As almost all the pans and vleis are parched long before the end of the dry season, there is a natural limit to the number of animals able to survive in the park. But boreholes sunk in recent years to provide water have created new centres for enormous concentrations of game throughout the year.

More than 1 000 floral species, including 230 different trees and shrubs and almost 200 grasses have been identified at Wankie. And in this province of the animal kingdom where there are 400 species of bird and 100 varieties of mammal, it is the elephant of which there are some 14 000, that dominates.

92

93

91 *Three giraffe gazing loftily from a woodland thicket seem to embody the characteristic feminine curiosity that is attributed to them by the Bushman.*

92 *Rhodesia's many wildlife reserves are sanctuaries for creatures of the water, land and sky yet it is the reptiles and larger mammals that usually capture most attention. However the wealth of insect life should not be overlooked: here butterflies mate.*

93 *Bold markings warn predators that this insect will not make a tasty meal.*

94 *Warthog have a roguish air, and this boar seems bent on mischief. His great curved upper tusks are a symbol of dominance to deter would-be rivals rather than to inflict actual harm. The short lower tusks are better suited as weapons.*

95 *The Arabs called the giraffe 'the one who is graceful' but at a waterhole it must adopt this ungainly splayed position to reach water. The giraffe's neck contains only seven vertebrae – no more than most mammals including man – but they are elongated to give this creature its impressive reach that allows it to browse at tree-top level.*

94   95

96 *A herd of elephant ambles in close formation towards a pan, the young shielded by the massive bodies of their elders. Elephants are sociable animals, herds looking to an old cow as their leader.*

97 *It takes 100 litres of water a day to slake the thirst of an elephant. These great creatures also have extravagant and wasteful feeding habits which have brought drastic changes to the Park's vegetation and there is much controversy as to the best way in which to deal with the problem. Some advocate culling to limit the size of the herds and therefore the amount of damage; others suggest that left alone, nature will herself provide solutions to the problem.*

98 *I'll scratch yours if you'll scratch mine . . . a pair of baboons groom one another. This ritual expresses three important aspects of the social behaviour of the baboon: dominance, tolerance and affection.*
99 *Marvellously limber and dextrous, vervet monkeys romp in the Park.*
100 *A mother sable keeps a careful look-out for danger as her calf suckles.*
101 *Fine kudu horns such as these are protected from trophy hunters in the Wankie Park.*
102 *Mainly found in the riverine north, waterbuck are scarce in other parts of the park.*
103 *Hood flared, forebody tensed for the lunge, a cobra rises to meet a challenge.*
104 *As the veld begins to dry, dwindling pans draw birds and animals to their muddy verges and nutrient-rich waters.*

102

103

104

105 *Reflections at a waterhole.*
106 *The life of the wildebeest is essentially one of continual migration dictated on one hand by their selective feeding habits and on the other by the fact that they normally drink once a day and are therefore tied to water. As the rainy season approaches, the great herds know instinctively that soon their summer grazing will be flushed with green and before the rain breaks they are on the move, sometimes cavorting in comic frenzy across the veld, at other times moving in single file.*
107 *Sometimes described as the clown of the veld because of its facial markings, the gemsbok is a fast, powerful animal with needle-sharp horns that it can use to telling effect.*
108 *The golden-breasted bunting is a common inhabitant of the trees of the savanna.*

108

109-112 *Crippled after breaking its leg in a hole, this wildebeest had been hobbling about for two days, continually harassed by three famished cheetah. The wildebeest could not have survived beyond a few more days, and the cheetah were unlikely to be able to kill it. These sleek creatures normally hunt smaller prey, depending on a magnificent sprint to overtake the fleeing victim. Before the cheetah goes for the actual kill by attacking the throat, the victim is often knocked over with a blow to the rump. Unlike the lion or leopard with their powerful jaws and heavily muscled bodies, the cheetah cannot break its victim's neck with a lunge at the back. On this particular occasion, even after a shot from a ranger's rifle had put the wildebeest out of its misery, the cheetah were unable to break through its thick hide and eventually had to approach their meal by the way of the anus and the soft flesh beneath the upper lip. No time was wasted, for cheetah are often driven from their own kill by lion or hyaena and in this case the sheer size of the meal meant that they could not drag i away to a secluded spot and eat at leisure. They are fastidious about the parts of the animal they consume but in the process make a great mess of the carcass, disembowelling it without care and then taking great chunks of flesh and bolting them down. Vultures had already begun to settle in the nearby trees and soon other scavengers would arrive. The cheetah di not consume a great proportion of the meat, nor did they return later to the spot to eat more, but as is their practice left the mangled remains to th scavengers of the veld.*

113-115 *The lion, having dined to satisfaction*
(113), leaves the kill to the scavengers. Within 18
hours of lions bringing down this buffalo in the late
afternoon, only the horns, skull, and a few scattered
bones and shreds of scraggy skin remained of an
animal that may have weighed some 700 kilogrammes.
During the night hyaena and jackal (114) took their
turn and by morning they had already consumed a
considerable amount; the jackals stealing tit-bits, the
hyaenas displaying their prodigious appetites and
speedy demolition of a carcass. Only the horns and
teeth escape their attention. Using massive premolars
they crush the bones, everything passing through the
digestive system except hair which is regurgitated. As
the air warmed the following morning so the next
creatures in the scavenging hierarchy arrived to
demand their share (115). Soaring high on the
thermals vultures soon spotted the kill and as the first
dipped its wings and began its descent, so scores of
others converged on the spot. Among the vultures, too,
there is a definite pecking order. Smaller than the
others and the first to arrive is the hooded vulture but
it is soon driven off by the much larger lappet-faced
which is best-equipped to tear open the carcass if the
ground scavengers have not yet made their mark. By
far the most numerous are the white-backed vultures
which jostle and shove to grab a share of the carrion,
even entering the body cavity to drag out the entrails.
And so the feast continues until eventually blow-flies
and maggots in the scraps attract smaller birds and
over a period of time even the horns disappear.

116 *Polished black hides gleam as a herd of buffalo thunder across a grassy plain.*
117 *Crimson and black, yellow and white, a saddlebill stork cuts an elegant figure while pacing with measured strides as it searches for frogs and other small creatures in the shallows of a vlei.*

118 *The secretary bird, strutting through the veld like a misplaced Dickensian lawyer's clerk, prefers to rely on its powerful legs to outrun danger, and only takes to the air as a last resort.*

119 *At sunbreak the ground hornbill's distinctive booming call announces the new day. These large birds spend most of their time on the ground, looking for insects, frogs, small reptiles and mice in the grass, only using their wings for short flights to a branch of a nearby tree when disturbed.*

120 *A male ostrich fans his fine feathers, not in a display of masculine vanity, but to increase his apparent size and discourage an intruder from approaching the nest.*

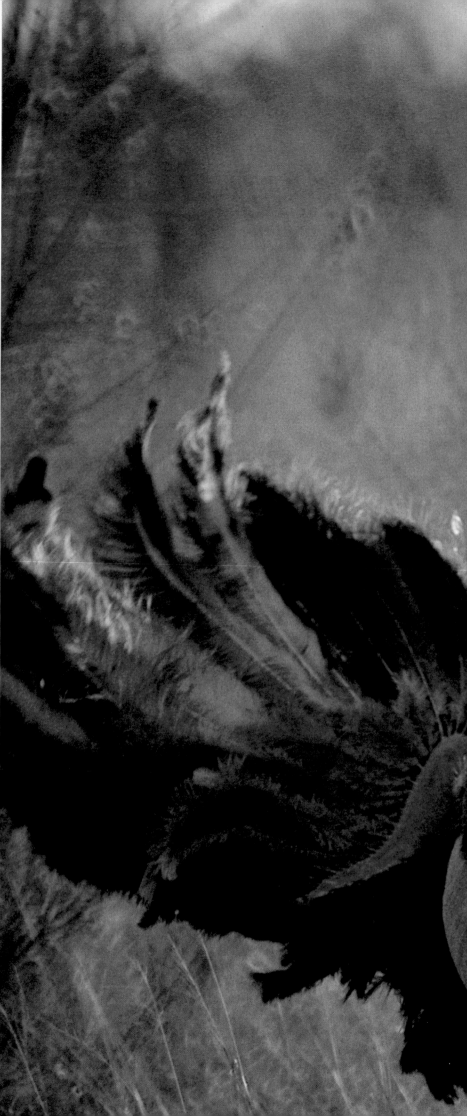

121 *Sunset in the Park.*
122 *A tree in the foreground breaks this view of the Park's largely featureless skyline.*
123 *Bones litter an open plain where, after the rains, game gathers in its thousands to graze the sweet grasses.*
124 *Tribesmen still venerate the baobab and it is a protected tree which serves a multitude of purposes. The fruit are a source of food, the skeletons of dead trees serve as grain storage bins, various parts of the tree are used to make traditional medicines, and when the land is gripped in drought rain trapped in hollows in the trunk provides water.*

124

Chimanimani is a word with a sound as evocative as the call of a bird, but as the name of a mountain range it is the legacy of a misunderstanding. When the first European settlers in these parts pointed it out and asked what it was called, the local people thought they were indicating a gap in the range. And so, the

CHIMANIMANI

mountains ceased to be called the Mawenje, meaning precipitous, and became Chimanimani, which means pincers. Although they lie towards the southern extremity of the lofty ridge of mountains on the Mozambique border, the Chimanimani are set apart, not only topographically from the interior, but also geologically from the rest of the Eastern Highlands. Composed of a different rock type and formed under dissimilar conditions, they belong to the aptly named Frontier System, which does not occur elsewhere in Rhodesia, except for a minor showing in the eastern foothills of Inyangani.

Rising to 2 438 metres at their highest point, they are the broken remains of an immense white quartzite massif that was thrust up against the unyielding blue quartzite of the Melsetter Plateau 1 600 million years ago by tremendous mountain building pressures from the east. Where these met, the white quartzite was forced up on to the shoulder of the plateau, folding, sheering and shattering in the process.

From a distance, the Chimanimani look as if they have been rounded, smoothed and burnished to a waxy lustre, which may be blue or grey, pink or cream, depending on the light. But on the summit and in the valleys of the thrust faults, chaotic assemblages of splintered rock recount the ancient story of that titanic clash. Grotesque gargoyle-like shapes recall the deep-water formation of the quartzite. Now covered with brown, russet, orange and deep-green mosses and lichens, bathed in swirling mists and aglitter with droplets left by passing showers, they seem still to be part of a submarine world.

Topographical and geological isolation has conferred a distinct ecology, in which lush green slopes, dotted with wild fig trees, lead on to the remnants of dense evergreen forests, hung with epiphytic orchids and 'old man's beard' and carpeted with ferns. On the upper slopes, aloes, proteas and golden everlastings splash the bracken with colour.

In a fertile valley that is reminiscent of English downs, facing the Chimanimani from the west, the first European settlers in this area under Thomas Moodie founded the tiny village of Melsetter, where the first tea estates in the country were established and which is today the administrative centre of softwood plantations covering 30 000 hectares.

But the old Chimanimani gap, the route used by the earliest Arab traders between the coast and the interior, is still only accessible on foot. The mountains themselves remain unscarred by roads, and the dark peat-stained pools and sparkling streams and waterfalls have a primeval aura.

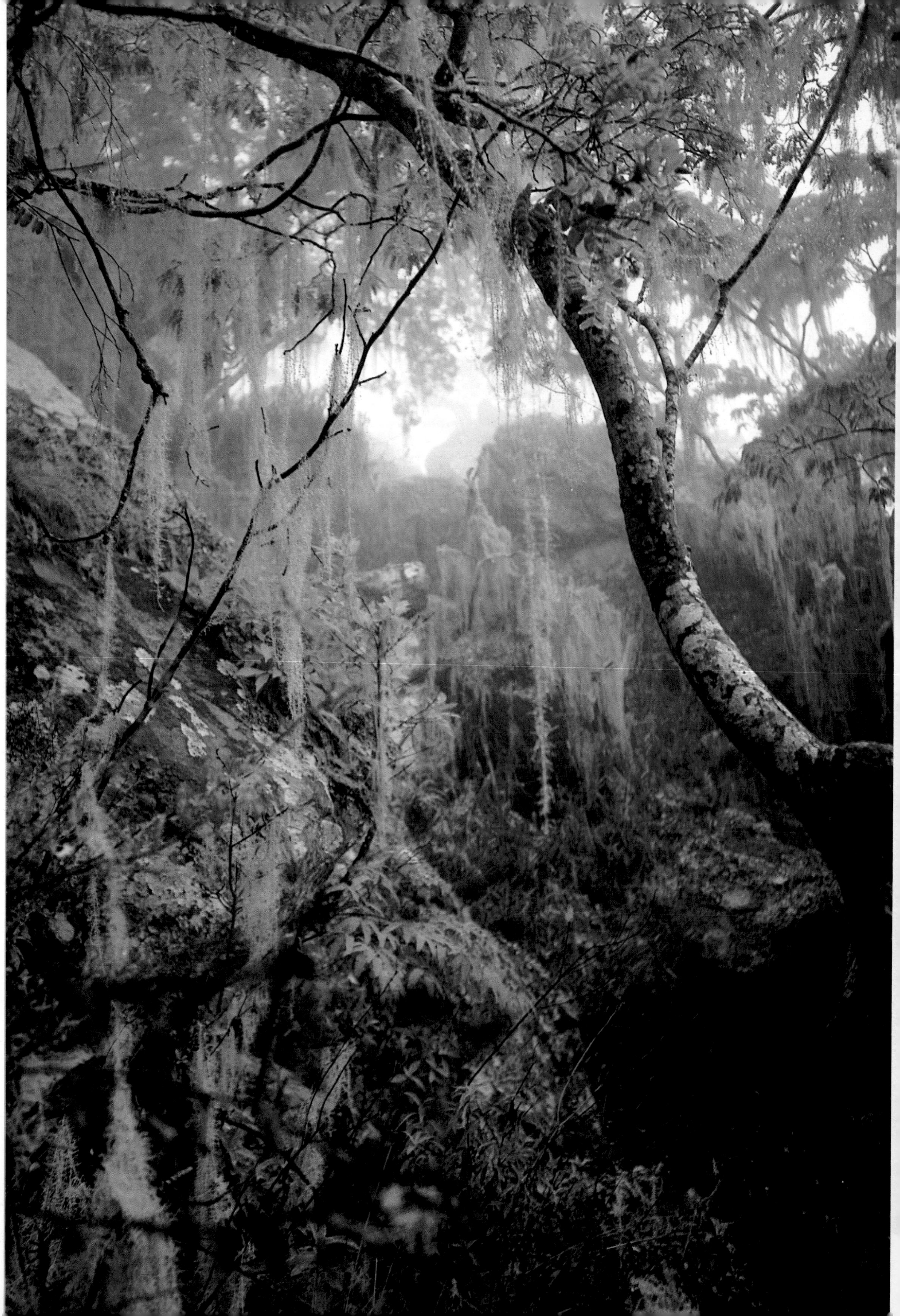

125 *Over 2 400 metres above sea-level a simple flight of imagination transforms the lichen-painted rocks into a coral reef.*
126 *Drifting mists and 'old man's beard' trailing from branches evoke an aura of Gothic romance.*
127 *A plant typical of the vegetation of the Chimanimani region where roads and motor traffic do not intrude upon the grandeur.*
128 *One of the many streams that tumble and gush along rugged courses through the Chimanimani.*
129 *An uprooted tree now jammed between boulders is a reminder that at times this dry watercourse is a raging torrent.*

127

128   129

130 *An otherworldly mountainland of weathered rocks daubed with lichens.*

131 *A chaotic jumble of broken rock remains as evidence of the immense power of the forces that created the extraordinary landscapes of the Chimanimani. Here eland, bushbuck, blue duiker, klipspringer and leopard make their homes, and purple-crested loeries, malachite sunbirds, mousebirds, francolins, laughing doves, larks, trumpeter hornbills, swallows and swifts enliven the brooding silences.*

132 *Looking back from the western ascent towards Melsetter. In these valleys European settlers successfully planted tea and softwood forests.*

From 50 kilometres away, spray hurled into the air by the Falls appears as smoke columns 500 metres high on the horizon. Nearby, the earth trembles and the water boiling in the chasm below beats like some great primeval drum. *Mosi oa tunya* – the smoke that throbs – was the name given them by the Lozi of the Zambezi's

VICTORIA FALLS

flood plains. Later tradition translated this more evocatively as 'the smoke that thunders', while David Livingstone, the missionary-explorer who first astounded Europe with news of their discovery, rendered it more prosaically 'smoke sounds there'. Mentioning that the local people called them *Shongwe,* which he interpreted as 'seething cauldron', Livingstone says he 'decided to use the same liberty' as had the Lozi and named them the 'Falls of Victoria . . . the only English name I have affixed to any part of the country'.

To attribute the discovery of the Falls to Livingstone smacks of ethnocentrism and has little in its favour. Stone tools indicate that primitive man lived there 40 000 years ago and various black tribes dwelt in the vicinity for centuries before the Europeans came. Although Livingstone's wanderings took him only twice into the territory of present Rhodesia, he stands today in a larger-than-life bronze effigy on the Rhodesian bank, looking out towards the island on the lip of the Falls from which he first glimpsed them in 1855.

The Falls cascade over a massive basalt shelf 1 700 metres wide and over 100 metres deep. When the river is in flood it creates an almost continuous sheet of water but at the height of the dry season it is possible to cross the lip except at the Devil's Cataract on the Rhodesian side where water always surges through the 30-metre gap.

The spray thrown up from the Boiling Pot descends in a perpetual shower over a narrow strip of rain-forest along the bank, where vervet monkeys chatter among vines in African ebony, wild fig and sausage trees. Sunlight, piercing yellow- and green-fringed apertures in dark upper foliage, projects back-lit palm fronds, ferns, red haemanthus and white ground orchids on the surfaces of shallow pools, and rainbows dance in the wet grass.

As the sometimes sentimental Rhodes wished, a 200 metre steel bridge was built over the Zambezi 'where trains as they pass will catch the spray from the Falls'. Symbolically, a recent major conference between the territories it links was held here, high above the chasm that divides them.

Below the present Falls, one can plot the Zambezi's zig-zag course as it has retreated along intersecting faults in the black basalt. And as it gouged a path so it created in ages past several falls quite as spectacular as the one today. The gorges are all that remain of these ancient falls but it is a continuing process and already there are signs that the river's torrent is working back along weaknesses in the rock to some distant future when there will be a new falls upstream and the Victoria Falls as we know them will join the march of silent gorges.

135

136

137

138

133 *The nineteenth century artist-explorer Thomas Baines marvelled at this foaming turbulence which he called the 'Leaping Water'.*

134 *John Chapman recorded in his journal after visiting the Main Falls with Baines in 1862: 'At our feet fell the towering mass of milky water into a chasm . . .' from which 'thick clouds of vapour came flying up fast and fierce from within the lowest deep.' And, in keeping with the images of the new industrial era, he added that the sound of the Falls could 'only be equalled by the united efforts of a thousand busy steam mills'.*

135 *Above the Falls the Zambezi flows broad and calm until it reaches the sheer lip where the waters are instantly transformed into an angry torrent.*

136, 137 *Below the Falls the river boils and churns down narrow gorges.*

138 *At the Devil's Cataract the river has begun to erode a weakness in the basalt and will, over millennia, work its way back along this fault. The line of rapids in the background marks the next major fall-line to which the river is gradually retreating, repeating a pattern seen in the succession of gorges below the present Falls.*

139 *The interplay of light and water creates a spectacle at once dazzling to the eye and deafening to the ear. In the mist that hangs perpetually about the Falls rainbows dance. Even at night, if the moon is full, the colours of the spectrum gleam in a lunar rainbow.*

140, 141 *Makishi dancers perform wearing traditional masks of painted bark cloth and dress of hand-crocheted fibre. These dances were originally intended to instruct young boys during the lengthy initiation schools. The insistent drumming, the clapping and singing rise to a frenzy as the dancers enact set pieces. The highlight of the dance centres on Nalindele, a character representing a young and wilful girl who shuns domesticity and seeks excitement. A skilled male dancer performs this rôle, first taunting the audience with what is to come and then, as excitement builds up, approaching two ten metre poles set fairly close together and linked at the top by a rawhide thong. Nalindele, after annointing her toenails with a magic potion, then scales the precarious structure and performs with breathtaking agility high above the spellbound crowd.*

142 *At a farm near the Falls crocodiles are specially bred for their valuable skins. Scenes such as this are a favourite tourist attraction. Five percent of all crocodiles hatched here are returned to the Zambezi from where, in many places, they had completely disappeared.*

141
142

143 *Patches of brightly-lit undergrowth dappled with pockets of deep shadow produce the sharp contrasts that give a distinctive quality to the light in the Rain Forest.*

144 *This sign in the middle of the Victoria Falls Bridge marks the border between Rhodesia and Zambia. Although officially closed, the goods trains between the two countries have continued to run.*

145 *Fifty years after Livingstone first saw the Falls, Rhodes's dream of a railway link with the north became a reality with the completion in 1905 of a steel bridge spanning the gorge between the two territories. Built 111 metres above the river, it was the highest bridge in the world at the time and was mounted on rollers to absorb the expansion and contraction of its girders.*

144

145

The transformation of Rhodesia in fewer than 90 years from a land of virgin bush, subsistence cultivators and cattle-herders into a scientifically farmed industrial country has laid the economic foundations for transition to a changed political future. Ironically, more than a decade of trade sanctions, designed to break the

TRANSITION

economy, actually broadened and even strengthened these foundations.

Diversification in industry and an enforced search for new markets encouraged rapid growth. Today the infrastructure is impressive: more than 3 400 kilometres of railway line link the cities and larger towns to the railway systems of neighbouring countries. A network of almost 6 000 kilometres of tarred roads and 72 000 kilometres of gravelled roads covers the country. Existing electrical power sources can supply the 7 000 million kilowatt hours consumed yearly.

Mineral production has continued to grow at an ever-increasing rate, with asbestos, chrome, gold, copper and coal accounting for all but 10 percent of the total value. Coal reserves of some 6 000 million tons assure the future of a vast energy source, while high-grade chromite reserves of over 600 million tons give the country long-term strategic importance. In the face of adversity, manufacturing industry almost doubled production, with increases in metal, textile, other mineral and food products ranging from 160 to 120 percent.

Agriculture is the main industry, in which production has nearly trebled over the past decade. Before UDI, half the earnings came from tobacco, but diversification promoted maize, wheat, cotton and sugar to major crop status. From producing barely eight percent of its needs, the country is now self-sufficient in wheat. Cotton production has increased eight-fold. Tea, coffee, citrus, deciduous fruit, groundnuts, soya bean and oil seed have become profitably established. Improved animal husbandry provides all domestic beef, dairy and pork product requirements and two-thirds of the demand for mutton.

The 90 years of growth since the first settlers arrived have not altogether effaced the colonial origins which impressed a pattern of interaction between settlers and the indigenous peoples. In Rhodesia today there are some seven million people of whom 95 percent are black. Five million are still linked to the subsistence economy in the designated tribal lands that occupy almost half of Rhodesia. Upward of a million are employed in urban and white farming areas. Population pressure intensified demands for the more fertile white farm lands, and those who had been drawn through their labour into building the industrial society found that they were denied many of its benefits. Their discontent, articulated as a call for political change, backed by the force of arms and the support of the international community, became irresistible.

After a 90-year interlude, Rhodesia is caught up once again in the broad sweep of African history. Today, the heirs of the Monomatapas, the Rozwi mambos and Mzilikazi, in new political groupings, compete for a richly enhanced legacy.

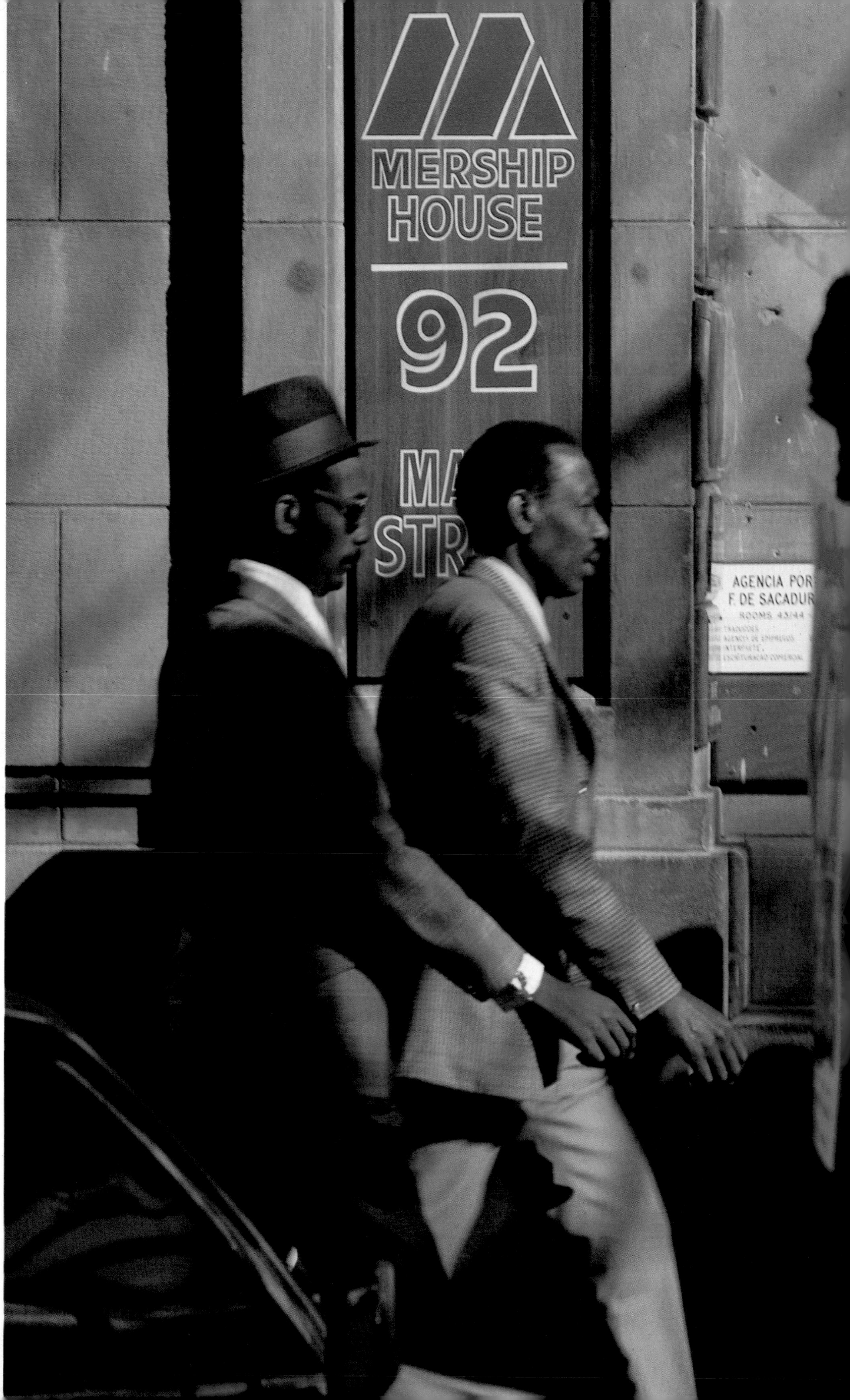
MERSHIP
HOUSE
92
MA
STR
AGENCIA POR
F. DE SACADUR
ROOMS 43/44

148

149

146 *The capital city Salisbury spreads gracefully over what was, not quite 90 years ago, an empty plain. Here, high on the central plateau, the Pioneer Column hoisted the Union Jack in 1890 to found Fort Salisbury.*

147 *Although the bulk of the black Rhodesian population is still rural, they look for the future to the towns and cities where recent years have seen the emergence of an articulate black élite.*

148-150 *Close on 600 000 people live in Salisbury but the pockets of green that intersperse the built-up areas, the broad streets and pavements, the quiet restaurants, parks and pedestrian malls make this a city for the people as well as a place for machines and commerce.*

150

151

151 *Punters in the 'gold ring' at Borrowdale Race Course where major events attract crowds of 20 000. Horse-racing is a national pastime in Rhodesia, with a tradition almost as old as Salisbury itself: the first race meeting was held here in 1892, a mere two years after Fort Salisbury was founded.*

152 *A welter of commercial signs above the heads of Saturday morning crowds in one of Salisbury's busy streets.*

153 *Commuters share a bench at a city bus stop.*

152
153

154 *Almost half the entire white population of Rhodesia live in Salisbury's 138 suburbs where residential holdings are often large and low labour costs have enabled these suburban dwellers to surround their homes with well-tended gardens and ornamental trees. In the more affluent areas such as this one, a private swimming-bath is a social asset which a fair number have acquired.*

155 *When it is spring the jacarandas bloom, casting a gentle canopy of mauve flowers over the avenues; this schoolboy celebrates the season with a tune on his mouth-organ.*

156-160 *White Rhodesians inherited the British love of sport, whether for team games like rugby or cricket, or something more individual like sailing or sliding on one's belly down a slope of smooth wet rock. Tea and cake at the clubhouse are as much a part of the tradition as the game itself.*

157

159

160

161 Harare, well-established in a cloak of green, is one of Salisbury's 12 African townships which between them accommodate almost half a million people. Nearly every house is surrounded by a carefully cultivated vegetable garden.

162 Township life has a style and tempo all of its own. Here the traditional way of life is rapidly modified by innovations from other cultures and as the traditional bonds loosen so they are replaced by new allegiances, goals and incentives.

163 It may take time for a family to make the transition in lifestyle demanded by a move from the country to the town. This adaptation far transcends simply changing a village hut for a brick-built township house; it strikes at the fundamentals of living such as family ties and obligations. Wages suddenly put new material possessions within the grasp of many and the transistor radio, a powerful medium for new ideas, is often one of the first purchases.

164 *Older people feel less at home in the urban townships and tend to return to their tribal homes when they can no longer be economically active.*

165, 166 *For thousands of township people traditional medicine men and healers still play an important rôle. The urban version of the herbalist has adopted something of the professional image of his Western counterparts, the pharmacist and doctor.*

167 *This game introduced to Africa centuries ago by the Arabs is still played by people in the townships and rural areas, but crown-corks have replaced the stones and a table-top the bare earth on which it used to be played.*

168 *Soccer is the most popular sport among Africans, and when the home team is defending its crown or challenging for the honours, supporters turn out in their thousands to cheer it to victory.*

165

166

167

169, 171 *The café and the pub are the focus of small-town social life and the clearing house for local news. Farmers from the surrounding districts come here to find companionship and to discuss the events that are shaping their futures.*

170 *All the major roads in Rhodesia were formerly strip roads, like this one where etiquette demands that passing cars each relinquish one strip, leaving a churn of dust in their wake. Today only 68 kilometres remain, the rest having been replaced by fully-tarred roads.*

172 ,173 *For many Rhodesians in small towns the tie with the land remains strong and there is something of the pioneer spirit among them.*

169

171 172

174

175

174 *In the lovely Shamva district – called after the wild fig-tree – smoke billows from a nickel refinery.*
175 *A worker at the Wankie coke ovens which have an output of 400 000 tons a year – enough to satisfy the demand of the entire domestic market and that of adjoining Central African territories. Wankie is the site of the world's largest known coalfield and it yields a high-grade product. At the end of the 19th century a lone prospector, Albert Giese, heard of the deposits from local Africans who described them as 'black stones that burn'.*
176 *The Rhodesian Iron and Steel Company's steelworks near Que Que where some of the country's immense iron ore reserves are refined.*
177 *Belching flames symbolise Rhodesia's remarkable economic growth over the past 90 years. Her mineral reserves are impressive and economic sanctions have in latter years encouraged diversification and rapid development of resources.*

178 *Rhodesian tobacco is among the finest in the world. Here Rex Morkel checks by smell and feel the quality of his crop. Formerly tobacco accounted for 50 percent of agricultural production but it became difficult to market after trade sanctions were imposed because the superior quality of the crop made it relatively easy for experts to identify its source. Subsequently half the land under tobacco was given over to other crops.*

179 *Coffee is an important new crop in the Eastern Highlands.*

180 *Cotton, hardly cultivated in Rhodesia 15 years ago, has risen to fifth place in Rhodesia's agricultural 'top ten'. In terms of foreign earnings it ranks second only to tobacco. Rhodesian cotton farmers now claim to have achieved the highest yields in the world.*

181 *Mainly a subsistence crop among rural Africans, groundnuts have never been successful as a large scale crop.*

182 *Sunflowers make a substantial contribution to the vegetable oil requirements of the domestic market.*

181

182

183

185

183 *Prime beef on the hoof. Six million head of cattle are easily able to satisfy the domestic demand for beef and dairy products and still supply export markets with a substantial amount of meat. By selective breeding, Rhodesian cattle farmers have produced successful strains adapted to sometimes adverse local conditions.*

184 *Sugar has become a major crop since the Sabi-Limpopo irrigation project transformed the dry south-eastern Lowveld in 1958. In this area the Kyle and Bangala dams supply water to the thriving Triangle and Hippo Valley Estates.*

185 *The art of tea-picking has been acquired by many of the local people who work on the large tea estates at Chipinga and Inyanga and on a pilot project along the Moçambique border.*

186 *Irrigation, which makes a winter crop possible, has contributed significantly to Rhodesia's self-sufficiency in wheat.*

187 *For over 40 years the silver arch of the Birchenough Bridge, rising 90 metres above the Sabi River, has been a landmark to travellers between Fort Victoria and the Eastern Highlands.*